# What Happy People Know

**If you are depressed, sad or worried read this book to understand how to:**

Rediscover your mental health
Feel more enthusiastic about life
Enjoy quiet inner confidence

John A. Doorbar

# WHAT HAPPY
# PEOPLE KNOW

Bibliografische Information der Deutschen Nationalbibliothek:
Die Deutsche Nationalbibliothek verzeichnet diese Publikation in der
Deutschen Nationalbibliografie; detaillierte bibliografische Daten sind
im Internet über http://dnb.dnb.de abrufbar.

Herstellung und Verlag: BoD – Books on Demand, Norderstedt

ISBN: 9783756879717

## To Michili

*Thank you for your love and support*

*in so many ways*

## Einstein

*The most important decision anyone can make
is whether we choose to believe we live
in a friendly or a hostile universe.*

# Contents

# Testimonials

### A simple, deceptively profound book

**What Happy People Know** us an honest, simple, deceptively profound book. John Doorbar beautifully uses personal stories, including his own experience of depression, to show readers how the human experience works. I most highly recommend this book. The insights John writes about are available to you, too!

*Amy Johnson, Ph.D. Author of The Little Book of Big Change: The No-Willpower Approach to Breaking Any Habit and Just a Thought: A No-Willpower Approach to End Self-Doubt and Make Peace with your Mind*

### An Uplifting Book

In this beautiful, uplifting book John not only shares his own story; he hands people the key. Will they use it as he did?

Many say miracles don't happen. John is living proof.

Dr Jack Pransky, author of numerous books including Somebody Should Have Told Us; Seduced by Consciousness; Modello; Hope for All; and many more...

### Practical Wisdom

John Doorbar has written a colorful, glorious book of practical wisdom to inspire hope and creativity in all of us. His personal journey from despair to a life of love and light is pure inspiration for us all.

Steve Chandler, Author of Time Warrior and 40 books on coaching and helping people achieve their dreams.

## Positive change

"John explains the fundamental insights of awakening to show you who you really are.

However, beware! This book could have a positive change on your life"

Michael Fritsche, Curriculum Developer I, John Deere GmbH Co. KG

## Change

In a clear and light-hearted way, John unveils the change in his experience of everyday life and moods, thanks to the understanding of the Three Principles as described by Sydney Banks.

Thank you, John!

Dr. Angela Scarano, medical consultant and psychologist who specializes in working with children.

## The right message at just the right time

John Doorbar's new book offers the right message at just the right time. As the entire world has plunged into a pandemic, our lives have been severely disrupted and, in some cases, destroyed. While we may be feeling the repercussions for generations, one immediate and widespread effect has been an alarming increase in mental health issues. Depression has never been more prevalent, and John understands this first-hand. His book goes deeper than the usual empty platitudes, and instead focuses on practical solutions. Get the book for you or someone you love.

Lou Bortone, author entrepreneur and video marketing specialist, who works wonders if you need marketing films.

### Inspiring

I have witnessed John's transformation from fighting depression to embracing exploring and thriving. I'm thrilled that he is sharing his story about what has helped him. Inspiring!

Dr. Ana Melikian, who helps high-value clients create transformational businesses worldwide.

### Condensed Wisdom

This is a gem of a book written by a gem of a human being, who like Job, wrestled with Life until it was his own. This book is the condensed wisdom from a classic hero's journey where you can see the gift humbly revealed behind decades of depression. This book is a gift to thousands of others who suffer from the relentless "Leprechauns" in their own heads, whispering in the background a repetitive, negative story that just isn't true.

Justin Perkins, Founder of New Edge Coaching. Justin is transformational coach who supports companies and their executives to achieve their true potential.

### The book had me laughing and crying...

"An open, honest and touching story of a man's transformation from despair to wellbeing. The book had me laughing and crying, feeling John's struggles and insights.

I too had a huge transformation from a life of misery and alcohol addiction. The 3 Principles pointed me to my innate wellbeing and gave me a new life of peace and freedom from addiction. The book will inspire you and point you to your own innate wellbeing. In John's words.

"This stuff works." It's the truth.

Sally Wyse, 3 Principles Professional Practitioner

## Improved knowledge and understanding

While reading this book and getting to know more background information, I was able to look at some of the challenging phases of John's life from a different angle. Together with the profound knowledge and examples he gave in each context, I have generally learned a lot about the 3 principles and other related topics. Some of it made me rethink my own experiences and knowledge, and others were so clear that they immediately helped me to understand better and broaden my perspective.

Christiane Neuss

## Inspired by hope and a sense of possibility

"Inspired by hope and a sense of possibility, John Doorbar brings us "What happy people know." His newer found peace of mind and joy after many decades of distress and trying to get better is what fuelled him to share a simple understanding of how people function at the most basic level. As I was reading this book I often felt as if we were having a cup of tea in the backyard, his sharing is down to earth, friendly and often humorous. "

Gabriela Maldonado Montano, 3 Principles Expert

This book contains advice and information relating to health care. It should be used to supplement rather than replace the advice of your health care professional. If you know or suspect you have a health problem, it is recommended that you seek your physician's advice before embarking on any medical program or treatment. All efforts have been made to assure the accuracy of the information contained in this book as of the date of publication. The publisher, author, and editor disclaim liability for any medical outcomes that may occur as a result of applying the methods suggested in this book. Any use of the information in this book is the reader's sole responsibility. This book is not intended to diagnose or treat any medical condition and is not a substitute for a physician.

# Timeless Insights

Throughout time, human beings have experienced insights that spontaneously and completely changed their behaviour and their lives, bringing them happiness they had previously thought impossible...

Achieving mental stability is a matter of finding healthy thoughts from moment to moment. Such thoughts can be a second away.

The Missing Link by Sydney Banks

## A Book of Stories

This is a book of stories which I very much hope will help you to see something new.

*"Metaphors, stories, musings speak to the heart, not to the brain. Listen with your heart, that is where we all find inner truth"*

Dr George S. Pransky - Life is a Metaphor

# Letter to My Readers

What on earth are these Three Principles? As you open this book you might be thinking this to yourself. What is this 3 Principles stuff all about? "Some weird new-age psycho-babble garbage?"

If that is what you are thinking, then we have a lot in common. Because that is exactly what I was thinking when I first heard of these principles. So what are the these principles?

The Three Principles are a way of understanding where our experience of life and feelings come from. People often look questioningly when they hear this sentence. Let me begin with a simple example to illustrate what I mean.

## The good news about happiness

This good news gave me hope, especially when I felt unhappy and depressed. People we call happy do not always feel happy.

I always used to think that being happy or being unhappy was a continual life-long state. You were either one or the other. However, this is not true. How we feel in life changes quite often and our feelings depend on our thinking.

Happy people sometimes feel unhappy too. But they do not think about it very much. They do not see their unhappiness as **affecting** who they are deep-down. They do not think of themselves as being permanently unhappy people. The do not identify with their temporary unhappiness and low mood. They know that the bad feelings will pass if they do not hold onto their stressed, hectic and overwhelming thoughts.

My dad was like that. He knew that he was fine just the way he was. He did not try to change. He just waited for his innate happiness to come back. Then he got on with his life once again in his own jovial, inimitable way.

These are the things my dad used to say when he was feeling low. *"I am not really feeling quite myself - "I am not quite on form today."*

*"Dad, can I help you to feel better?"* I used to say when he was feeling *"out of sorts"* as he called his feeling. *"No, I will be alright, John. I am fine. I just need a few minutes. Just leave me alone and I will be back to normal soon."*

## Mental health

Mental health is not about trying to change. It is rather to do with really understanding deep down that we are all OK exactly as we are. Our moods go up and down but our basic nature is to be happy and peaceful. Little kids do not feel happy all the time but when they feel unhappy they do not think about it too much. They just forget about it and go back to enjoying themselves.

If our basic nature is to be happy you might be asking, why on earth do I not feel happy? How on earth can I feel happy? I sincerely hope that the answer to this question will become clear as you read through this book.

## Let me begin with a simple example

This short story has a worrying beginning and a happy ending. It even has a P.S. (a postscript) at the end.

A dear friend of mine, Barbara, lives about 30 kilometres away from us in Germany. She has, over the years, become a close family friend of Michi and me. (Michi is my lovely girlfriend and partner). I quite often call Barbara to see how she is getting on. I had not heard from her for about 8 days. So, on a Saturday morning in June about four years ago something strange happened that made me think. Barbara did not answer the phone. And she did not call back.

During this period, I went through 6 levels of thinking.

**Step 1:** I thought to myself, "that is no big deal." "Just give it some time. Maybe she has just gone out to do some shopping." Then I forgot about it and went for my regular Saturday run.

**Step 2:** Towards mid-afternoon on the same day, I still had not heard from her. I called again. No reply. Oh, I now noticed that my thinking was starting to get a bit noisy, "I hope she is OK. I am sure she will be fine. Maybe she has gone for a drive. Drivers are sometimes crazy in Germany. They drive much too fast. Oh, she will be OK. She can look after herself...and so on."

**Step 3:** I noticed myself getting a bit more concerned. The thinking was getting to me. I was starting to feel my worried thinking. I started to pace around my flat a bit like a lion in a cage. So, around 19.00 I called again and again. Now my thinking started to go into overdrive. My imagination took over.

**Step 4:** "Maybe she has fallen and hit her head on her bath and was lying unconscious in her bathroom in a pool of blood. Or perhaps someone had broken into her flat." My thinking was getting darker by the minute. I hardly got any sleep that night and woke up at 6.30.

**Step 5:** My thoughts were still going round and round in circles and getting worse. I noticed that my blood pressure was going up.

**Step 6:** I telephoned her once again. Barbara still wasn't at home. So, I took my jacket and picked up her keys (She had given me a copy of her keys in case of an emergency)

I got in the car and drove much faster than usual over to her flat. The drive was not very nice, and my head was full of lots of crazy thoughts. When I got there, I put the key in the lock and opened the door. I was greeted with my friend hiding behind the door holding a very big dictionary in her hands. She was ready to bash me on the head as I came in. As you might have imagined, we were both surprised when she recognized that it was me! And I was relieved. Barbara smiled at me and asked me what on earth

I was doing there at 6.30 on a Sunday morning. I explained what I had been thinking.

This story ended happily. Barbara had been at home the whole time. Her phone had been out of order for 6 days or so. She had not been able to hear the phone ringing even though, from my end of the line there had been a normal ring tone.

In this situation with Barbara, I had "thought myself" into a state of panic.

This book is about how our own feelings are created from our own thinking. We do not consciously do this. It just happens. These feelings are so strong that they feel real. And these feelings are what we experience in the world as our personal reality. This story taught me that my experience of an event (i.e. how I feel) is created 100% by my thoughts.

P.S. There is a postscript to this story.

From 10th November-12th November, 2022 I was fortunate to attend a wonderful course with Robin Charbit and Ken Manning, two of the leading practitioners in the "understanding of human experience" which this book is based on. On day two of this course, I called Barbara to see how she was getting on.

I had called Barbara 4 years earlier and had created the horrible scenario in my mind which I have explained above. This time I had a new thought, which I had not had 4 years previously, "oh that is nice, I thought – I am sure she has gone for a run and is enjoying herself in the lovely November sun." I felt great that she was having fun!

This was the same event, an unanswered telephone call, both on a very early morning on sunny, summer Sunday, separated by 4 years. But I had a very different experience – the first very negative, the second extremely positive.

With this new thought my experience had changed. And this was a completely different feeling for me. The experience which I had was being created in my mind by my incredible power to generate my own experiences.

This is how we experience our own personal world, and this is what the Three Principles are about.

## If you feel depressed

As you read this book you will see why it can be so useful and important to know about this if you are feeling sad or depressed. And as you will see, I have known what it feels like to be low and depressed. So, I can imagine where you are coming from and how you could be feeling.

## A different experience of life

The Three Principles are remarkable in that they are easy to grasp and once grasped have the power to change lives. They helped me personally to experience my life differently.

Although my outside life has not changed very much, I have felt very different. I feel much freer and more relaxed. I do not take things as seriously anymore. I go with the flow of life. Not always. But a lot of the time.

For me, this new feeling is worth its weight in gold. And I never imagined that this change would ever be possible.

It is strange but we never really know that good things can come out of what, at first, seemed such a negative experience.

Nevertheless, being depressed can be deadly. Literally.

I know well what it feels like to be depressed. I have personally "done that" and got the T-shirt. This is the reason why I have written this book. If I had not experienced being sad and depressed, I could never have written it. I now see this as something good. Something good can now come out of my previous sadness and unhappiness. I hope that I can help other people to see that their life can get better, even if they think it can't.

## A parable

There is a great Chinese story that shows us how good things can come out of something bad. Maybe you have this great parable before. It is called "The Farmer and his Horse."

## The farmer and his horse

There was once a farmer in ancient China who owned a horse. "You are so lucky!" his neighbors told him "to have a horse to pull the cart for you!"

"Maybe," the farmer replied.

One day he didn't close the gate properly and the horse ran off. "Oh no! What a disaster!" his neighbors cried. "Such terrible misfortune!"

"Maybe," the farmer replied.

A few days later the horse returned, bringing with it six wild horses. "How fantastic! You are so lucky," his neighbors told him. "Now you are rich!"

"Maybe," the farmer replied.

The following week the farmer's son was breaking in one of the wild horses when it kicked out and broke his leg. "Oh no!" the neighbors cried, "Such bad luck, all over again!"

"Maybe," the farmer replied.

The next day soldiers came and took away all the young men to fight in the war. The farmer's son was left behind. "You are so lucky!" his neighbors cried.

"Maybe," the farmer replied.

So, what is the point of the story?

Whenever we interpret a situation as being a 'problem' or an 'opportunity' it shapes the way we feel. This shapes the way we respond.

The story of the Taoist Farmer shows that we can never know how a situation is going to turn out. There are no intrinsic 'opportunities' or 'problems': there is only what happens. We never know what to expect.

I never thought I might feel better. But I really do.

Good things can always happen when you least expect them. I think this "Maybe" story gives us hope that we never really know what is going to happen.

Things can change and we can change.

When I talk about the Three Principles, which you will read about in this book, I often get a blank stare. Eyes glaze over. The shutters go down. And most people change the subject very quickly or move on to speak to somebody else.

That's why I'm writing this book for you – to explain, in the simplest way I can how I understand them so you too can feel their transformative power in your life as I did in mine.

Let me take you back to 1969. A little village in northwest England, called Elworth, where I lived as a child.

## Unanswered questions

When I was about eight years of age, I was very curious. I watched the world around me and I had a lot of questions. Many of my questions were easily answered. But one question remained, persistent and unanswered. Why I wondered did I feel totally different after experiencing exactly the same event? Sometimes I felt sad and sometimes I felt really fine. This did not make any sense at all. How was it possible for me to have two different reactions to one identical event?

For example, when I played football on a Saturday morning, against another school team, either we won, or we lost. Sometimes I was devastated by our loss. I felt terrible. Yet, the next time, when we played and lost, I didn't mind at all. I felt just fine. So, what was the difference? Why did I feel differently when I experienced the same event?

It took me forty-eight years to find the answer to this question. It took me virtually my whole lifetime to unravel the answer to my persistent question – to grasp something which I didn't understand before. And what I finally understood changed whole way I thought about my life and how I experienced it.

**The missing link - To feel anything we must think something**

My penny dropped. I had a spark of insight. I suddenly understood that feeling and thinking are like two sides of the same coin. How I thought about an event impacted how I felt about that event. This was the missing link connecting the things that happened to me and how I felt about them.

In other words, I experience events and then I have thoughts about the event, and I experience these thoughts in the form of feelings. How I feel about my life, at a particular time, and what happens to me in the world outside is one hundred percent colored by how I think about what is happening to me.

This process is not unique to me. We all experience the world like this, in just the same way. This is what I am going to share with you in this book. But please do not take my word for it. See for yourself whether this is the truth. Test it for yourself. And then make up your own mind.

> *"Listen with a kind of a fresh mind.*
>
> *Listen with a fresh mind,*
>
> *without prejudices,*
>
> *without fixed formulas."*
>
> By Anthony De Mello

What you will read about in this book explains how some people have outwardly terrible lives. They experience the deaths of family members poverty, hunger, oppression, racial hardships, and much more - Inwardly though, they are able to experience inner peace and live an enjoyable life. The reverse is also true. Some people have everything materially any person could ever wish for - fame, fortune, family, a Ferrari and a loving spouse - and yet they decide to jump to their death from a very high building.

So what's the difference here?

The difference is how people *experience* their lives. How people *experience* their lives is wholly dependent on their thinking. These are the thoughts they have while events are happening to them in their lives. By understanding, even just a little of this profound truth I have been able to act differently.

When I had the choice, I decided not to jump off an extremely high building. In other words, this flash of insight changed and saved my life. It is not about trying hard to get better. This might sound crazy, but it's true. It is not about goal setting and trying out yet another life-strategy method. It is not about taking yet another self-improvement course. It is not about using your willpower to change your ways. It is not about working harder, faster, better, more effectively.

It is about seeing our true nature.

## Connecting the Three Principles

I'm often asked about the interconnection of Mind, Consciousness and Thought that make up the Three Principles. There is a deep and perpetual connection between them. When I first heard these Three Principles, I scratched my head and didn't get the point.

So, I developed my own way of understanding the links between Mind, Consciousness and Thought that became very helpful guide.

## How the Principle of Thought works

First, let's explore the Principle of Thought and how it works. Thought enables us to experience our life on earth.

## My mum and the rugby match

My mum and dad both loved rugby. One freezing Saturday, winter morning I was playing in our weekly game. And our mum and dad were both on the touchline as always. My mum always got tremendously excited during the games. She was really into the action. At half-time, we had a short break and our traditional, if somewhat unusual snack of, half an orange. I went over to my mum and dad to see how they were getting on and whether they were enjoying the game. But when I felt my mum's hands they were absolutely freezing. They were even colder than mine.

But the interesting thing is that my mum had not even noticed that her hands were icy cold. She only felt the cold in her fingers when I mentioned it to her. In other words, when her thoughts were on the game, her reality was telling her that her hands were at a normal temperature. When I mentioned how cold they were, her thoughts changed. It was at that moment that she felt the "reality" of her cold hands.

## How the Principle of Consciousness works

Now let's explore the second Principle – The Principle of Consciousness. I will use this example of my mum to show the power of Consciousness. When we experience things in the world, we have thoughts about them. Sometimes, these thoughts just move through our minds and leave just us as fast as they arrived. When this happens, we do not experience them as "real."

On other occasions, we have an experience (exactly as in the previous situation) and again we have thoughts about that experience. How did Consciousness function at the rugby match?

Earlier I told you the story of my mum and the rugby match. She was so involved in the match and enjoying it so much that the thoughts she was experiencing were presumably about the match. She was really "into it," like anyone who might get engrossed in a great film or book.

These thoughts gained their own reality because the Consciousness element enlivened them. My mum did not inject Consciousness into these thoughts intentionally or knowingly. Consciousness was just present, and it brought my mum's thoughts alive.

Let us contrast this with her experience at half-time. Here I felt her hands and said, "Blimey mum, your hands are absolutely freezing." I did not realize that my comment might have had an effect on the type of thoughts which she was experiencing. Now these new thoughts were being experienced by my mum and they were now being brought alive via Consciousness. Her thoughts were new, so the experience she had was also new and different. Now, the reality she experienced was, "Wow, my hands are really cold,"

My mum really felt this "coldness." It was real to her.

I did not intend this to happen when I drew her attention to her cold hands. And neither did she. Consciousness was happening behind the scenes. It was automatic.

In a nutshell...

## Watching the game

Here my mum was having thoughts about the great game like - "the game is exciting." A "sprinkle of Consciousness" brought these thoughts to life. My mum consequently experienced an exciting game.

## At half-time

Here my mum was having thoughts like "my hands feel very cold." A "sprinkle of Consciousness" was added again. So the result was that she experienced the coldness in her hands and fingers. She felt that her hands were bitterly cold.

Please remember, as I mentioned earlier, that thoughts and feelings are inextricably linked together. This process is happening all the time to everybody and everywhere. This is how we all experience our lives. However, we often do not notice it.

**Do you want to find out what is happening behind the scenes?**

The idea of this book is to help you to see what is happening behind the scenes. It is not the intention that you actively try to change anything. When you get a small insight as to what is happening then you might well have a different experience.

Change happens on its own, often unexpectedly when we have an insight which allows us to see behind the scenes.

I'm not saying that things outside in the world are just illusions. They are real objects and ideas. What I am saying is that how we experience these objects or ideas depends completely on the thoughts which are attached to them.

## My Dad the beekeeper

My dad loved bees and kept hives in our garden. Whenever he saw these bees, his eyes lit up. And he loved to talk about them – especially about how important they are to our environment. I knew this too. I knew that bees are important. However, When I thought of bees my eyes didn't light up. Quite the opposite. A frightening feeling of panic went through my whole body. All I had to do was think of bees and I was in a state of terror. This is the power of Consciousness – the power to transform our thoughts into very strong feelings.

Unlike my father, I couldn't think of sweet honey or stand in awe of the miracle of pollination, or even feel sadness at their threatened extinction. All I could think about were the times those bees had stung me when we played football in our garden - painful memories that resurfaced every time I saw a bee. So Consciousness is the power that our thoughts require to come alive. How the Principle of Mind works

In this book, I'm going to be using Mind in a special way. Mind is the energy in the universe which Albert Einstein described in his famous findings.

This Mind is the formless energy and the intelligence behind life. You could say that it's the life force that gives life to our world. It is that special something that allows us to live and thrive in our bodies. It is that source of energy that powers us throughout our lives and keeps our bodily systems working.

But this energy doesn't only impact our bodies. As Einstein discovered, this energy is everywhere. It is omnipresent. The Principle of Mind provides the stage on which events and actions can occur. It is the backdrop where everything happens.

## The Three Principles and other mental models

As you know, many models exist, all of which attempt to explain our thought processes and behaviour. Psychologists, psychiatrists, and philosophers offer support to try to help people with their mental struggles. I could list about four hundred different types of mental models and therapies that all aim to change peoples' lives. However, most share what is, in my opinion, a very unhelpful way of viewing their patients or clients.

I must add though that some of these models really do help people, at least some of the time. However, many of these models share a very unhelpful starting point. When these practitioners treat their clients, their starting point is that there is something wrong with the client. They view their clients as broken. They begin with the presupposition that people are ill, rather than beginning with the presupposition that people are healthy and have an innate state of mental health. Do you presuppose people are ill or do you presuppose people are healthy and have innate mental health? Whenever I went to so-called "mental health" professionals, they treated me as though they were "mental illness" professionals. By that, I mean that they always asked me what was wrong with me. This did not help me, and I believe that it doesn't help most people who are feeling rubbish about their life. The last thing depressed people need to focus on is how rubbish they are feeling. But a question from a therapist like, "Mr. Doorbar, just tell me why you think you have got so many problems," is not exactly helpful. A question like this can be deadly.

The difference between these traditional therapies and Sydney Bank's discovery of the Three Principles is extremely important. So many of the therapies out there presuppose that people with mental challenges are ill – that they need to be treated and taught strategies to get through life in a slightly happier way.

Sydney Bank´s discovery, on the other hand, demonstrates that people have innate mental health within them that has often been covered over or hidden by their life experience. This innate health is always there and can be rediscovered. This is a true model of hope.

And that's what you'll discover in the pages of this book. You will not only read about my own stories but also about ways in which the Three Principles have helped others in typical situations where people often have difficulties. For example, when they have problems in relationships or with stress or in coping with money. Towards the end of the book you will read stories of how the Three Principles have helped people in these challenging areas

The ideas of Mind, Consciousness, and Thought might seem tricky to understand at the start. My goal is to show you that these ideas are extremely practical and if you look at them with an open mind, they have the power to change your experience of life for the better. This is what the Three Principles did for me.

With love and my best wishes on your way to good mental health,

John

**Takeaway**

- ☑ We see things differently depending on our thinking. Some people love bees. I respect them. I do marvel at the work they do but I prefer to admire them from a distance.
- ☑ "There is nothing either good or bad but thinking makes it so." William Shakespeare.
- ☑ The missing link - To feel anything we must think something.

**Resources**

Dr George Pransky, Life is a Metaphor 2022 – A wonderful little book of metaphors which beautifully reveals the power of the Three Principles.

# *About This Book*

*"The Three Principles is not a self-improvement course, trying to improve what is. Rather, it is understanding the nature of what is."*
Dicken Bettinger

This book is a unique and deeply personal story of my long, recurring struggle with depression and how I finally stepped out of the darkness and into the sunlight.

I credit my more peaceful and much happier life to one man, Sydney Banks, and his unique insights and understanding. He called what he had learned and experienced "The Three Principles."

After dozens of self-help courses, hundreds and hundreds of books, and multiple sessions with a wide variety of doctors, therapists, and coaches, it was the Three Principles that restored my mental health. Actually, I had never really lost my innate mental health. It had just been hidden from view.

This is not to say that I do not have bad days. I do. But they are not nearly as bad and they do not last so long. And when I am in the middle of a difficult period I know somehow that this state is not permanent. It will pass. Everything is in a state of constant change. **Everyone has bad times even if they are normally very happy. As Sydney Banks said, "Life is a contact sport"**

Sydney Banks lays the foundation of his understanding of life on his website.

My name is Sydney Banks. Over thirty-five years ago, I had a profound spiritual experience that revealed to me three, long lost, divine principles that are the foundation of all human experience.

I was an average working man, not searching for truth or wisdom or even aware of much beyond my day-to-day life. Why me? I'll never know, but my life became a mystical journey where people suffering mental anguish of every kind came to hear me speak or read my books and quickly found mental health and true peace of mind. Now many of those same people, mental health professionals, and lay people alike are helping thousands of others find the peace and happiness they have been searching for.

On this site (sidneybanks.com) you will hear many stories of hope and discovery from ordinary people, mental health professionals, inmates in prisons, people who have left their addictions behind for life, and more. My hope is to give you as deep an understanding as I can of the three principles of Divine Mind, Divine Consciousness, and Divine Thought.

I invite you to explore the Three Principles with me through the pages of this book. Here you will find not only my interpretation of and experience with the Three Principles but also the stories of others whose lives have also been changed for the better.

The first part of the book includes:

- The Prologue,
- The Origins, and the
- Aim of this book

They will give you important background information and lay the foundation for what is to follow.

# Overview of the book

### Chapter 1

Chapter 1 entitled the Search is all about my early struggles and the countless unsuccessful and expensive remedies I tried over a very long period. I wanted so much to dispel the black clouds of depression that so often had hidden the sunshine from my life.

### Chapter 2

Chapter 2 describes my tentative steps as an early learner of the Three Principles.

### Chapter 3

Chapter 3 takes a deep look at what happiness is, and what it is not.

### Chapter 4

Chapter 4 is an introduction to the Three Principles.

### Chapter 5

Chapter 5 takes a deeper look at the core fundamentals of the Three Principles to illustrate them through stories. In this way you will see many examples of how these Principles have helped other people.

## Chapter 6

Chapter 6 focuses on the valuable lessons I learned and how the Three Principles have had a big influence on many areas of my life.

## Chapter 7

Chapter 7 takes a detailed look at how the Three Principles help people with specific and practical challenges in their lives.

The Three Principles have made a big difference in my life and thousands of other people. I am healthier, happier, and often filled with a feeling of lightness.

As I have mentioned, this is very different from how my life was before. I really hope that by seeing something special in how these Three Principles function you will come to enjoy things more and feel better about life.

# *Prologue*

*"Foster peace in your own life and then apply the art of peace to all that you do."*

Morihei Ueshiba (the founder of aikido)

This story begins with a little boy. The backdrop of this book is the story of a little boy who started happy, healthy, and full of wonderful possibilities in life. However, all too soon he began to believe an illusion that he was not worth anything.

**Illustration 3**

He is sitting in this photograph on the bottom left - the guy with the cool hairstyle. The year was 1969. He was eight years old – a significant year in his young life – it was the year that he first started to feel inadequate and a waste of space. That little boy, of course, is me. This book is a chronicle of a difficult journey that took me from that early happy boy through years of negative thoughts. To find a cure I read countless books and attended courses by many well-known people. A journey with many insights.

It is possible to experience happiness, joy, satisfaction. It is possible to finally stop feeling sad, depressed, and inadequate. Or to have far fewer horrible feelings.

The key to feeling better again is not some fancy technique. I have been very lucky to finally understand and see what is happening in the background, behind the scenes. I still have my ups and downs. But that is life. Ups and downs are nothing to do with being depressed. Life is a contact sport. The understanding I achieved helped me and I hope that it helps you too.

What we all need is hope. This book is in fact a story of hope I am now going to take you on this special journey with me.

# The Origins

## Personal and practical

This is a very personal book. It is also a very practical one. It is largely based on my own experience of life.

## Everything begins as an idea

I never actually intended this to be a book at all.  Its origins started as just an idea. Four and a half years ago I was sitting in a seminar – one of many I attended in Spain over several years - when I was moved to start writing down my notes and impressions on what I had learned. I planned to give a small section of my "notes" as a thank you to the seminar leaders who had inspired my notetaking and had helped me to get my first tiny insight into the Three Principles. They were also to become my friends and I am very grateful for that. You will be meeting these two very special people later in the story.

So that idea took seed in my mind. I started writing. I continued. And that little present for my teachers turned into something bigger and more life-changing – it changed into a book.

"All we are peace love and wisdom and the power to create the illusion that we are not."

Dr Jack Pransky

# Aims of this Book

*"We all live in our own thought-created reality. If we don't think something, it does not enter OUR reality. It doesn't matter if it's "there" or not; the only reality we can see and experience is the reality we create via our own thinking."*

Sydney Banks

## In the beginning

I had struggled quite a lot with depression for most of my life, from the age of about 10. All I ever really wanted was to be happy. Even though I took course after course, attended countless workshops, listened to hundreds of hours of speakers offering advice – nothing really helped

## A compelling truth about life

Finally, quite by accident, I stumbled on an understanding of life called The Three Principles. The Three Principles Foundation offers an introduction to this remarkable life-affirming truth. In the process, we will learn about Sydney Banks, the man who was the first person to get an insight into the Three Principles.

Here is how the website describes the very special experience which Mr. Banks had. In 1973, Sydney Banks, an ordinary working man, experienced a spontaneous and profound spiritual enlightenment. His experience uncovered three foundational Principles; elemental principles that create and govern the human experience: **Universal Mind, Universal Consciousness, and Universal Thought.** His unparalleled insights into our true nature are creating a renaissance in the field of psychology. They have opened the door to an authentic science, grounded in principle, and based on the most salient facts about who and what we are.

These Principles are the key to a divine mystery and a spiritual understanding that has evoked a paradigm shift in our understanding of human psychological functioning, and as such, in our approach to mental health and healing.

From Three Principles Foundation website

## Recognizing the Three Principles

It's now more than five years since I saw something special in The Three Principles. This small insight changed how I experience life. And I wanted to write about my understanding of these Three Principles. I wanted other people to see how they can change the way they can experience their lives.

One problem I encountered right from the start was in trying to explain in simple and understandable terms what these Three Principles are.

Another problem was to show how anyone who sees how these The Three Principles work can experience their life differently.

## First aim is to explain the Three Principles

My first goal in this book is to explain the Three Principles in terms that anyone can follow and understand. To bring The Three Principles more alive I have put some of the ideas which I write about into pictures, drawings, illustrations and cartoons. I hope these visuals will help to illustrate the lessons you will read about.

## Second aim is to document great examples

My second goal in this book is to bring together all that I have learned from my very special teachers. This includes some of the great examples and stories they have shared. These examples are like "gold dust" because they help all of us appreciate how the understanding of the Three Principles has affected, normal people like you and me.

The journey you will experience is unique to you. Some people think that the insights they will gain involve extreme out-of-the-ordinary experiences. And for some, this is what happens. Other people on the other hand have small insights and little by little these mini-insights help them to see and experience things differently.

## Third aim is to illustrate how life can change

I also want to demonstrate how these Three Principles appear in all areas of our lives and all disciplines. My life journey, experience will be different from yours – and that doesn't matter. The Three Principles can affect your life as powerfully for you as they did mine. I was lucky to get a place to study at a famous British University where I could read Theology.

I was fascinated by the university and loved playing rugby and rowing. However, it has only been recently that I returned to my study of Theology after a long absence. I credit my renewed interest and fascination in my Theology studies to Sydney Banks' great insights. I see the Three Principles as an understanding of how we experience our lives and I can now see clear spiritual links with Theology. Sydney Banks was the first to say modestly that what he was teaching was nothing new! But for thousands of people who were suffering from a distressing life, they saw something new. And then their world changed.

What Sydney Banks has managed to accomplish through his life-changing and life-reaffirming understanding is to help people tap into their inner well-being by seeing something new in their lives via these Three Principles.

## Touching every part of life

This understanding crosses many disciplines - theology and spirituality, psychology and traditional religion, quantum physics, literature, and art. This understanding also has an effect on performance in sport and business. Its effects can be dramatic.

Ever since I learned how the Three Principles work, and I have seen them appearing in many aspects of my life. I have spent over four years researching some of the most enlightened spiritual leaders as well as other recognized visionaries in history. I have also studied the lives of contemporary experts and scientists who have written about psychology, epistemology, religion, physics, medicine, and of course, the Three Principles themselves.

Ultimately my goal is to present a user-friendly and comprehensive guide to these Three Principles which helped me so much. They now still allow me to experience my life in a new way.

## What this book is not about

I want to state clearly that this book is not about many of the 'feel good,' or 'feel better' pieces of advice offered in so many contemporary self-help books. Neither is this book filled with instant tips and tricks. You won't find any recipes for living a perfectly happy life twenty-four hours a day, seven days a week. I won't be writing about the latest craze, method, formula, or 'must do' series of life-affirming exercises.

In this book, we are going to be contemplating the Three Principles of Mind, Consciousness, and Thought and their relevance to how we experience our lives.

## Why write another book on the Three Principles?

After all, there have been so many excellent books written already about these Three Principles which describe this new understanding and reveal the mystery of how our experience of life works. So why write another book? That is a very good question.

## A new way of seeing

I have read most of these great books about the Three Principles. I'm not going to reiterate what they've said. I'm not trying to compete with them either.

I am writing through a personal lens hoping that you will feel different. I am going to share my story of how my life changed for the better. By allowing yourself just to sit back and quietly reflect on what I am writing about, I really hope that you will also find yourself living a happier life. These renowned authors and experts have seen something new.

It is this "new way of seeing" which is the thread that is woven through all disciplines. It is my hope that by the time you turn the last page in this book you will also gain some insight. And a new way of seeing what your own life can become. Almost all self-help literature has to do with trying harder. Do more. Go faster. Be more structured. Et cetera et cetera et cetera.

The Three Principles do not work like this.

People often get insights into their lives when they are just not trying. Insights often happen when we are in the shower, for example, or on holiday or while daydreaming.

I will always remember a lovely story which Dr. George S. Pransky told at a Conference in London.

A man in the audience asked him how to best understand the Three Principles. He answered by saying that it is possible to increase the chance of seeing something new by being calm and relaxed.

## A butterfly on your shoulder

People are charmed and delighted when a butterfly lands on their shoulder. But the butterfly only lands when we are calm. This is the state we need to be in to see something new.

**Takeaway**

☑ Relax and allow your mind to settle like a butterfly might settle on your finger when you are still.

☑ Change is possible. Have trust and never give up.

☑ This understanding is not about tips and tricks.

**Resource**

Dr George S. Pransky - Life is a metaphor

Dr George S. Pransky -The Specific Breakthrough Discoveries of Sydney Banks

# CHAPTER 1
# The Search

What are the three principles of consciousness according to William James? These are his thought.

1. Every thought tends to be part of a personal consciousness.
2. Within each personal consciousness thought is always changing.
3. Within each personal consciousness thought is sensibly continuous.

William James also considered the "spiritual self" and saw its link to thought. He also made a very perceptive and predictive comment.

*"Someday someone will find principles for psychology and when they do, it will change the field to a philosophy and a science and in turn it will help millions of people."*

William James

Houghton Library (Public Domain)
William James (sometimes called the father of psychology)

## Searching for the depression cure

I was in a terrible state. I had been struggling to pull myself out of depression for years. To that end I had tried dozens of ways to stop these horrible low moods. I started looking for help when I was very young because I always felt that my "never-ending sadness" was not normal.

## Looking to a doctor for help

I went to a doctor when I was about 11 years old. She knew nothing about depression and prescribed drugs for me. Undaunted, I went to other doctors and they proved to be equally unsympathetic. They said I just needed to keep my mind busy and develop a good social circle of friends. Despite explaining to them that I already had supportive friends it was nevertheless hard for them to understand the problem I had. None of the medical practitioners I was taken to had ever experienced being depressed. For all their best efforts they failed to help me out of my low moods.

## The university 'cure'

When I was at University in Oxford, I took part in special sessions with a university tutor at

St John's college. His solution was to try to convince me that I was not as stupid as I thought I was. His attempt at making me 'psych myself' check out of a low mood did not really work.

## Neurolinguistic Programming (NLP)

There was also a course of neuro-linguistic programming I attended to alleviate my depression. The method was designed to help see things from a new perspective as well as to model others. I was excited and hopeful when I signed up for an advanced course of NLP in the United States with Robert Dilts, one of the leading NLP practitioners in the world. Even though the program has a massive following and receives testimonials from thousands of people it did not help me at all. I completed the programme, and I was as unhappy as ever.

## Powerful pills

Next came the antidepressant pills - SSRIs (selective serotonin reuptake inhibitors). Again, I felt no change in my level and intensity of deep sadness.

## Cognitive-behavioral therapy

I was getting desperate. Next, I attended cognitive behavioral therapy sessions (CBT), a method that has received a lot of favourable reviews. Unfortunately, I was not among those whose challenges were helped with CBT. My very low mood stubbornly persisted.

## The avatar worshippers

The group that later I called "the avatar worshippers" exposed me to one of the scariest things I have ever done. Ever.

The organization appeared to be involved in the mass hypnosis of over six hundred people. I happened to be one of them.

Thankfully, I escaped before any damage could be done. My depression was not gone either. It had not even diminished. The group's instructors laid the blame squarely at my door. They told me that it was my fault that my depression wasn't getting any better – it seemed that I lacked commitment to their treatment. That is what they said!

I left this crazy group of guru worshippers to look for another solution. I was still depressed. When I asked for my money back, they said, "Sorry but you are a very unusual case and you fall outside our full, lifetime money-back guarantee." So, I was still depressed and £3,000 poorer.

As you might have already guessed I would definitely **not** recommend the Avatar Guru Worshippers Course.

## The Byron Katie seminar

Next, I spent Euros 4,000 on a Byron Katie seminar after reading one of her books. The teaching focused on how to access your wisdom, which always exists within you, through a form of meditation. This course was another disappointment for me. When I left this course I felt even more disheartened than when I had arrived. I must say though that Byron Katie does have her heart in the right place. Her course was just not right for me at the time.

## Hypnosis

After this seminar I tried to relax with hypnosis, listening to countless CDs. Nothing changed.

## Family and friends

I often chatted to my family and friends as well as support groups like the Samaritans.

Here are some of the people who have helped. My mum and dad, my brother, Michi, Gabriela, Jack, Angela, Bill, Dicken, Paul,

Mark, George, Ken, Uli, and Christiane, Mick, Katja, Sheela and many more?

These chats helped me more than anything else, at least for short periods. One of the great advantages of feeling depressed is that I got to make lots of wonderful new friends.

## Mental health professionals

Next came a long line of mental health experts – psychiatrists, psychologists, therapists, and coaches. I entered into each therapy they prescribed with hope but unfortunately, none helped. And even worse, rather than my dark moods getting lighter, my bank balance was feeling much lighter.

I experienced no change after multiple sessions with several psychiatrists.

Then I had the misfortune to find a therapist who turned out to be particularly useless when it came to my mental health needs. He was dreadful.

"Can you tell me about your problems so that I can see how depressed you are?" This was the first question he asked me.

So I told him about my problems for the next two hours and slowly felt myself sliding into a very dark black hole. He kept asking me to describe in more detail, how badly I felt and with each detail, I felt worse.

After this meeting I felt my depression weighed a lot heavier than when I arrived. I never returned to this dangerous mental "health" professional. And thankfully, he never sent me a bill which I wouldn't have paid anyway.

Finally, I went to what I call a "woo-woo" therapist. According to the Miriam Webster Dictionary, woo-woo means dubiously or outlandishly mystical, supernatural, or unscientific. During our first session, she instructed me to watch the direction of her swinging pendulum as she asked for divine guidance from the underworld.

"How can we best treat John?"

This was her question to the spirits as she seemed to enter some sort of weird trance. It turned out that she was even more depressed than I was. We changed roles and I ended up listening to her endless litany of problems.

Before I managed to escape she offered to pay me for listening. Needless to say I did not accept her money!

Then I did a course of treatment with six different coaches none of whom knew what to do with me. One very generous, and well-known coach even gave me my money back.

## Running as therapy

I also heard that running helped to reduce depression and that keeping healthy was even more effective than these dangerous and powerful SSRI drugs. So I made a "crazy" deal with my coach, Steve Chandler, a wonderful coach from the United States. I pledged that I would run every day for a year. I was so desperate that I got up early and ran for 365 days straight. I think even Steve was surprised at my determination. I never took a day off from my jogging regime and even appeared at the door of my brother's home after running 10 miles on Christmas morning. Understandably, he thought I was nuts. I thought that maybe my brother was right.

Having tried all this, I still couldn't outrun my depression.

## The work cure

I became convinced that work would keep my depression at bay. And so I threw myself into my job. I worked non-stop. I tried to keep myself so busy that I had no chance of thinking of anything else. This helped my depression slightly, very occasionally. But I couldn't keep up the frantic work pace and had to abandon my self-imposed work cure.

## The birds

Nothing I did worked. My thoughts circled round and round in my mind. Some of these thoughts were so horrible and scary that I experienced them as huge black crows circling, swooping, and attacking me, like those in the Alfred Hitchcock film "The Birds." Massive flocks of aggressive birds attacked other people and they were also attacking me.

For me, these horrific scenes in my mind were much more real than any Hollywood movie could ever be. My "birds reality" was a great example of the power of Thought which was being brought alive by Consciousness. I was somehow experiencing feelings of terrifying black birds. Not surprisingly, this experience did not help my sense of well-being.

## Transcendental Meditation (TM)

After the "Birds Drama" I turned to TM (Transcendental Meditation.) And TM was great in helping me to relax. I practiced TM diligently every day - 23 minutes in the morning and 23 minutes in the evening for five years – a total of 1,825 days. I have recently started doing TM again regularly and it really helps. It is based on solid research on how the brain and mind work and it is highly effective in reducing blood pressure.

I have included a great TM book on the list below.


I guess you could call this degree of regularity either dedication or desperation. I even attended a TM Siddhi course where people were supposed to learn how to fly.

Sadly, my attempts to fly never got off the ground.

All in all, Transcendental Meditation was another attempt to rid myself of my state of depression. TM did help me to relax a lot and I can really recommend Transcendental Meditation.

**Transcendental Meditation has many benefits**

Manic tendencies

I also have known times when I have felt very strong fluctuations in my moods. When I have a deeper understanding of where my feelings come from (I will talk about this in depth later in the book) then I am more able to objectively see what is really happening in my life.

## Highs and Lows

I have felt very "high" and that I could achieve anything. After this, sometimes I have slipped down into the depths of negativity.

After I started to understand that my feelings are directly linked to my thoughts, it was easier for me to just "sit and wait" until I came to a more balanced state. Sometimes it is better not to do anything. Our thoughts are continually changing and when we know this, we are more optimistic that our situation will change as long as I do not hold on to my thoughts.

They continually and naturally come and go.

## An important tip

Please do not make big decisions or changes when you are "high" (manic) or "low" (very unhappy).

For example, do not buy a house of flat. Do not change your husband or wife.

Do not make big financial investments (for example - in lots of shares).

Do not tell your friends that you never want to see them again.

The roller coaster feeling can be exhilarating and very scary. I personally prefer to keep my feet on the ground.

When we are "not balanced," i.e., too high nor too low, then we have a tendency to do things which we might regret later.

It is always great to have a friend who will give you honest feedback. I have been very lucky because my dear Michi has always been prepared to let me know when I was behaving in an overenthusiastic or weirdly energetic way.

It took me quite a long time to learn these tips for myself.

By reading about this here I hope you will understand where these manic feelings (tendencies) come from. When you know where these feelings come from (your thoughts) it is easier to guide yourself away from situations which might otherwise get you into trouble

## Astrology

Then I tried astrology. My star sign suggested that I was, or should have been, relaxed and easy-going. Nothing was further from the truth. I remained decidedly tense, anxious, and down-in-the-dumps.

I did briefly consider other "spirits!" If I had not been so level-headed, I would have headed directly for those other spirits housed in our drinks cabinet when I got back from work. Thankfully, I didn't.

## Natural "feel better" remedies

I did my research and decided to try St John's Wort. No joy. It didn't help but it did cost me an arm and a leg – lots of cash.

## Here I am adding up the cost of all the courses I attended

Is this the end? I had spent more than(about)275,000 Euros - which amounted to all my savings - on various costly seminars, hundreds and hundreds of self-help books, dozens of programs, and even "magical potions."

After all these attempts to climb out of my very low moods the only thing I had to show for it was an empty savings account. In my flat there were cupboards full of pills and potions, and shelves groaning with "feel better" books that never lived up to the promise of their titles.

I was desperate. I was so desperate that I even started going back to those overpriced workshops that had failed me the first time. How crazy is that?

Finally, in my desperation, I thought about ending it all, by jumping off a very high building. Luckily, I did not act on those destructive thoughts. I did not go ahead with this plan because I thought my parents and friends would be upset and would have to clear up the mess I had left behind – the literal mess (lots of blood and all) and all the rest that the tragic suicide of a loved one involves.

So, I just stopped. I stopped searching for a way to live a normal, happy, satisfying life. I stopped searching for a way to rid myself of my seemingly never-ending depression.

### Turning to beer

Actually, as an avid rugby player at university I always felt that beer did not really count as alcohol. I guess it served as a type of medicine, no matter whether we won or lost.

So as far as I could tell I just had this final option – and I took it. I just started drinking lots and lots of beer instead. I bought a case of beer a week and regularly drank three or four bottles a day.

I got fatter and fatter. My blood pressure started to rise due to a combination of the beer and the stress my thoughts were causing. It felt as if the effects of my thinking were becoming "embodied" in my physical body.

Not surprisingly, with this continual and very real "virtual reality horror show" playing over and over in my head, I could not sleep. My health was starting to suffer. Seriously.

I luckily met a very good friend at this time. One day she said that this drinking was not good for me and "kindly" poured my beer down the sink. I was not so happy about this. But maybe she saved my liver. I had tried quite a few things to turn myself into a happy person. I only wanted to enjoy my life. And none of my attempts at feeling better worked. I was stuck.

**One Beer Too Many**

## The end of the road – or a fresh start?

In my view, living requires more courage than suicide. I had run out of ideas. Run out of money. Run out of hope. I was at the end of my road. But what I hadn't counted on was the fact that life can surprise us. And life finally did surprise me and offered up a unique solution designed to bring me "out of the darkness and into the light.

**Takeaway**

☑ Choose your guides and mentors really carefully
☑ I can warmly recommend TM (Transcendental Meditation)
☑ If you feel down and if you can, then talk to a friend or empathetic family member or find someone who understands about the things I write about in the book.

**Resources**

How Life Works by Andrew Matthews
A beautiful and deep book with great illustrations

**Question/point for reflection**

It is not a good idea to believe everything you think.

### CHAPTER 2

# Hopeful

*"The thoughts which are fed with Consciousness and attention are the ones which grow."*

John's reformulation of a lost quotation

## Hopes raised

And then I found The Three Principles and hope for the end of my depression soared once more. From what I had read The Three Principles had already helped thousands of people to feel better and live happier. So, I thought, "Why not give it a shot! It can't be any worse than all the other "experiments" I've tried over the last thirty-six and a half years."

## Looking for happiness one more time

I might have been depressed but nobody ever accused me of being a quitter. If anything, my whole journey to personal healing was a testament to my persistence, dedication, and resilience. You might call it desperation! So I made the decision to go to my first Three Principles Conference which was being held in London.  And that's where I met Dr. Aaron Turner. My first impression of him was of how calm he was.

"Who are you, I asked tentatively. "My name is John," I said, introducing myself politely. "I'm Aaron" he replied. "Welcome and help yourself to coffee and biscuits, John" he continued and pointed me to the refreshment table.

"And may I ask what your role is here, Aaron?

"Oh, I am introducing the conference"

"Wow, you must be nervous," I said questioningly.

"No, not really and if I am…that is OK too, it doesn't matter," he said smiling.

He wished me a good day, then turned and went in the direction of the stage, where he was about to welcome 300 people to the event.

This baffled me. I couldn't make out whether he was nervous or not! He seemed unaffected by facing a room filled with this very large audience. I got the distinct impression that he would be fine no matter what – balanced, steady, and above all, happy.

I was fascinated, confused, and depressed. His positive and relaxed mood didn't make me feel encouraged. While I envied Aaron, I didn't believe that I would ever get to that calm and accepting state that he seemed to enjoy. felt that this Three Principles "stuff" and this conference in London was my very last chance to ever get better and so far, I wasn't impressed.- Little did I know how wrong I was.

As I took my seat, this conference was going to take my life in a very different direction.

**CHAPTER 3**

# Looking Deep Inside

## Johnny, the human skull

As I write this sentence, I have a perfect miniature copy of Johnny, a human skull, sitting on my desk. Johnny is smiling straight at me. Some people might consider it morose to have such a thing on my desk.

But for me, when I get too much into my head, I paint incredibly life-like pictures of a future disastrous event where everything is black.

When this happens, I look at Johnny. As I do this, I am reminded that we are all sitting precariously on a spinning planet flying around in the middle of nowhere. This phenomenon has been going on for billions of years and we have the privilege of witnessing this miracle personally, albeit for a relatively limited time.

## Playing a Good Act

I had always attempted to "find happiness" by playing a "good act." This did not work and left me tremendously frustrated, dissatisfied and sad.

It's not what's on the outside that counts.

Typically, when we think about our life experiences we feel that they are based on what is happening in the outside world. This is what I thought too. I was always striving to achieve something. Better, faster, wiser, richer. This "get richer" goal definitely did not work! I also wanted to be happier, become slimmer, cleverer, funnier, sexier. And this list went on. But I came to learn through The Three Principles that it's not our outer life, but our inner life that leads to inner peace. When you have inner peace, then you stop chasing achievement, satisfaction, wealth, wisdom, and joy.

## A prized academic life

And yet, when I look at my life, I was fortunate enough to be offered a place at Oxford, one of the most reputed universities in the UK, if not the world. I went to Keble College, read Theology, and was awarded an Oxford degree which I was very proud of.

My life at Oxford was not all about studying. I rowed. I was an avid rugby player and I had the honoured role as kicker for the team. In my second year, our rugby team won the University of Oxford College League. This was quite an achievement.

I was very confused though, because, on the outside, I didn't have such a bad life after all. I had never gone hungry as a child. I could go to the cinema when I wanted to. My parents were kind and loving. My brother, Richard was very supportive towards me. In other words, on the outside, my life was good. I was lucky. Lucky, but not happy, for much of the time.

For most of my life it was wonderful on the outside. On the inside though I was in what seemed like an endless low mood.

If I had "acted" just how I felt, then I would not have been able to do anything. I would have been completely immobilized – paralyzed inside the darkness that surrounded me.

## So, what did I do?

I put on a big act. I pretended I was alright. A few people saw through my façade, but most people thought I was fine, even normal. It turned out that I was a great actor.

And if the truth be known, during some of those very dark years, there were times when even I knew deep down that things were absolutely fine. But I deleted those good times from my experience. I was like a gardener who instead of pulling up weeds, pulled up the flowers which gave me a good feeling. I just cancelled out the good feelings which I so strived for. It was almost as though these good feelings had never been there.

So why am I telling you all this? For one important reason – my view is that if I can finally be happy and get some inner peace then anyone can.

## The happiness "secret" revealed

We don't really find happiness at all. What I'm writing about is to help you to see that you don't need to get anywhere at all to find happiness.

The secret? The big secret is that you already have what you need to be happy inside.

## The golden Buddha

There is a wonderful story of the golden Buddha that helps to illustrate the fact that you already have the prerequisites for a happy life inside you.

In 1957 a group of monks in Thailand were relocating their entire monastery. One day as they were moving a giant clay Buddha one of the monks noticed a crack in the clay. On closer investigation he saw there was a thin thread of golden light emanating from the crack. The monk picked up a hammer and a chisel and began to chip away at the clay exterior. Piece after piece of dusty old clay fell away to reveal the fact that that entire clay statue was actually made of solid gold.

Historians believe that the Buddha had been coated in a thick layer of clay by Thai monks several hundred years earlier to protect it from an imminent attack by the Burmese army. The Burmese army attacked, and the monks were all tragically killed, but the large clay Buddha remained intact and safe from the invaders. It wasn't until 1957 that this great treasure was discovered. The clay was chipped away, and the precious gold inside was revealed. What is the lesson which the clay Buddha teaches us?

As we go through our lives we collect "layers of clay," (clay here is a metaphor for everything which blocks our intrinsic human goodness) and this clay covers up our essential golden essence. I had tried lots of approaches which I've written about so far. As you have probably noticed, the one common denominator in all these methods was that they are all to do with fixing what is wrong with people. Inner peace doesn't work like that. We don't need to fix or do anything.

That's what I learned when I finally saw how we experience our lives via the Three Principles. I found out that I didn't need fixing. None of us need fixing.

What do we need?

We just need to know how life works.

**Takeaway**

- ☑ Look inside
- ☑ Remember the Golden Buddha
- ☑ You do not need fixing. Be yourself – Please do not pretend to be someone you are not. It is very stressful

**Resource**

**Invisible Power Ken Manning by Robin Charbit, Sandy Krot**

A great book which is extremely practical and explains the Three Principles in a crystal-clear way. This book is especially helpful for people in business.

These three experts also provide wonderful Three Principles Training.

### Chapter 4

# Meet the Three Principles

*"Sydney Banks' tremendous gift to the world was to bring simple principles along that would help people understand what Buddha was talking about, what Jesus was talking about everyone" Maslow, Carl Rogers, and William James. The Principles, if you look at them deeply, are behind what everyone is talking about. Everyone is saying that Thought is what creates your reality and that we are all a part of something much, much more."*

Ami Chen

## Meet Sydney Banks

My being able to write about the Three Principles is the result of the profound insights of one remarkable man. It is interesting that before he had the insight that changed his life and the lives of thousands of others. At first sight, Sydney Banks was a rather unremarkable man. Sydney Banks originally came from an impoverished suburb of Edinburgh called Leith. He moved to Canada and worked as a welder. He was not a particularly happy man, nor was he religious.

He was sometimes depressed.

One day, he had an experience that projected him into what could best be described as another dimension. Not like a new dimension in a science fiction film. But rather into a place where he saw a bright light and felt complete oneness with the universe.

There was more. In that flash of insight, he understood something very important. And it was the understanding that changed everything, both for him, and for the thousands of people who have been helped by his insight, including me.

This story might sound a bit weird. But from that day on Sydney Banks decided to leave his job and teach other people what he had discovered. He called his insights The Three Principles and spent his life teaching them to as many people as he could.

## What is a principle?

Maths was never my favourite subject at primary school. To this day, I recall seeing all the multiplication tables tacked on the walls of my classroom and feeling the fear of having to recite these tables by heart every morning.

There were also lessons in addition and subtraction.
And there was also long division.

"How much is two into eight?" Mr. Barlow my teacher would ask me while looking expectantly over his half-glasses.

I kept my head down hoping he would not choose me to answer. But he invariably did.

"8 divided by 2 is 4, Mr. Barlow," was my reply.

He smiled and asked, "Can 8 divided by 2 ever equal anything else?"

"No," I replied emphatically. This was only a really good guess on my part – I had no idea why not.

### 2+2 equals 4 – It always equals 4 - without exception

Mathematics and gravity both work via principles.

Only later did I truly understand this. You can't negotiate a principle. It doesn't matter how many times you do this simple arithmetical sum. The answer is always the same. So, what does my elementary maths have to do with the Three Principles?

It is a basic universal concept. Principles are non-negotiable. They are descriptions of how we experience our lives on earth.

When you drop an apple, it always falls to the ground, or on your head (, if you are standing under it, as in the illustration) when you drop it. It always works that way.

It is exactly the same with the Three Principles. They always work the same way. They work every time, whether you like them or not. Even when you do not know that these principles are at work, they still work.

## Introducing the Three Principles

1. Mind
2. Consciousness
3. Thought


Mind + consciousness + thought = reality


Mind, Consciousness, and Thought are the Three Principles that enable us to acknowledge and respond to our existence.

All human behavior and all structures are formed by this trinity of Mind, Consciousness, and Thought. There is an analogy in chemistry. In chemistry, two or more elements combine to create compounds. It is the same with the psychological elements of Mind, Consciousness, and Thought.

These three elements create the psychological mix that form our psychological realities.


## Healthy and unhealthy

A healthy mix generates feelings such as compassion, humility, love, joy, happiness, and contentment which are all rooted in positive thoughts. Hatred, jealousy, insecurity, phobias, and feelings of depression are all cocktails of negative thoughts.

All feelings derive from the power of Thought. This happens with both negative and positive thoughts. This sentence is worth repeating and emphasizing. So I will repeat it.

All feelings derive from the power of Thought. This happens with both negative and positive thoughts.

Mental functioning cannot possibly exist without the three psychological elements. They are the building blocks of all mental activity.

## Thought – the first Principle

Instead of giving an intangible theoretical definition of thought, I would like to share a practical and personal example to illustrate how thought plays a vital role in our lives.

"All you have to know is that everything is created from Thought; you don't have to know anything else."

### The "birth and near-death" of this book project.

This illustration is directly connected to this book which you are now reading. The idea for this project came to me in 2017 when I was sitting in a seminar in Spain.

I began the creation process.

Over the next two years, I collected ideas, worked out a structure, and wrote a few notes each day. Slowly the book took shape. I was encouraged and even elated.

Two years later, in 2019, I was scheduled to attend another seminar in Spain and I decided to give an early version of this book to two of my very good friends who were the seminar leaders.

I strongly respected their opinions and wanted to get some feedback. A project which had turned into a draft of a book had begun with a single thought – a positive thought rooted in discovery, creation, and sharing. I was feeling good.

And then came the flip side of that 'thought coin.' And the doubts poured in. Negative thoughts poured in. I had only completed about one-third of the book and still had two-thirds to finish

**My thoughts**

- *Can I actually finish this book?*
- *What if I don't finish this book after sharing my vision and draft?*
- *What if people think I'm showing off? Or worse, that I'm some kind of imposter? Loads of people have written books about the Three Principles. Why should I write another one?*
- *There are no new ideas in my book so what's the point of finishing it?*
- *I managed to overcome these thoughts and was able to complete a lot of pages between the training sessions.*

But when I was about to write the last part of my book these unhealthy thoughts returned – only this time they were much stronger.

This second wave of unhealthy thoughts was so crippling that I found myself thinking I couldn't finish the book. I told myself that it had all been a colossal waste of time – an exercise in futility.

The thoughts created strong feelings.

They were so strong that these thoughts had manifested in reality in the form of action. I shut down my computer, gathered up my pages, and decided to stop my book project completely. I was done. There would be no book. It was over. The desire to give up was powerful. Strong. Real.

The Principle of Thought was creating in my experience the feeling I was having. This was nothing personal. It is just how the Principle of Thought works.

I was very nearly seduced by my thinking.

My response to the thoughts being generated in my mind shocked me. As Dr. Jack Pransky has written, I was very nearly "seduced by consciousness."

My thinking slowly changed and I noticed a few positive thoughts. Here are a few of these new thoughts.

**My new thoughts**

- *Well, so what if most people do not like it.*
- *Maybe someone will!*
- *It might even help just one person.*
- *If one depressed person feels lifted and lighter by reading my book, then it will have all been worth the late nights and early mornings.*
- *And anyway, I wanted to give it to my friends, Gabriela, Jack, Sheela, and Katja as a thank you gift.*

New thoughts. New actions.

So, I opened my computer. My fingers started moving again. My book was back on track.

## Mind – the Second Principle

Mind is the power and energy of all things in the universe. It is a description of omnipotent and omnipresent energy.

What I find particularly fascinating is how the understanding, which came to Sydney Banks, weaves together a wonderful tapestry of truth.

Mind is the power and energy of all things in the universe. This truth has been known since the beginning of our existence as people on earth. In my view, Mind is an incredible and magical sea of nothingness that contains all the prerequisites for creativity and even for life itself.

This life-energy is part of the formless energy which is behind everything – all life, including all human life and all of existence. Now this all sounds very spiritual I know. However, what we now know from our study of science supports these ideas.

Let us look at Albert Einstein. This is what he said.

*"Every human mind has direct access to her/his experience here on earth, and the human mind always has access to its own spiritual roots from whence it came."*

Einstein

He described all matter as "simply" energy in another form. We, as humans, are also made up of matter and so logically it means that we are this energy - just in another form.

## Consciousness – the Third Principle

Remember the story about my mum at the start of this book? At the rugby match, she didn't even notice her freezing cold hands because she was enjoying the game so much.

But at half-time, everything changed. At half-time, I drew her attention to her cold hands.

This "attention" is called Consciousness. It is the component that gives life to our thoughts.

It was Consciousness which enabled my mum to experience her cold hands at the match.

During the rugby match my mum must have been having completely different thoughts. Her attention was not on here cold hands.

*She was probably having thoughts like...*
*"Now they're playing really well!"*
*"I hope John's team gets some more points."*
*"I hope John gets this conversion"* \*\*\*
*"Blimey, that guy is really fast"*

(a conversion is when a player kicks the ball between the posts. It scores 2 points. This was my task! An American field goal is a bit similar to a conversion in a rugby match)

It was these thoughts that were alive in my mum's mind during the game. These were clearly different thoughts from those which were in her mind when we spoke to each other during the break, at half-time. Her mind moved from the pleasure of the game to the discomfort of her frozen fingers.

Consciousness is the magical element that gives life to thought. Our Consciousness will determine how we experience what happens in our lives.

Consciousness can be compared to a spotlight projected from a torch. Whatever thoughts we put in front of the light (the Consciousness) become illuminated.

Consciousness is the magical element which gives life to thought.

If the spotlight from the torch of Consciousness illuminates trash - a symbol for horrible life experiences - then the trash is what we see and experience. Consciousness has no content in itself. However, it allows us to be aware of our thoughts.

If it illuminates a beautiful garden, then we see flowers in full bloom.

It is very important that we do not think incorrectly that Consciousness is something we do actively.

It is not something that we do.

Rather, Consciousness is working all the time, behind the scenes.

**Takeaway**

- ☑ Principles never change.
- ☑ New thought can generate change.
- ☑ All feelings derive from the power of Thought.

## Resource

**Life is a metaphor by Dr George Pransky**

I timed myself when I read this book.

It took me just 30 minutes to read this little gem.
In England we say that the best present come on small parcels.
This book is short and wonderful.

## Chapter 5

# Going Deeper

*"The mind is its own place, and in itself can make a heaven of hell, a hell of heaven."*

John Milton, Paradise Lost

## Stories and metaphors

Stories and metaphors are my way of personalizing and illustrating the Three Principles and how they have impacted my life – and how they can impact yours.

## How can we define the Three Principles?

When I first asked myself, "So, what are the Three Principles?" I found a simple and clear answer from Dr. Jack Pransky who said,

"The Three Principles are a way of helping people to understand where their experience of life comes from."

## What is reality?

Maybe this is a weird-sounding question. I certainly thought it was. When I heard it for the first time, I just shook my head.

Reality is what you make of the input you receive via your senses. Because we make up our own version of reality, we never really know what is "really real."

## The short story of Pablo Picasso

Let me just illustrate this with the short story of Pablo Picasso. A man named Kai is riding in the first-class cabin of a train in Spain and, to his delight, he notices that he is sitting next to Pablo Picasso. The man, who is interested in art, gathered up his courage to ask the great master a question. You are a great artist, but why is your art and all modern art, so screwed up? Why don't you paint reality instead of these distortions?" Picasso hesitated for a moment and asked, "So, what do you think reality actually looks like?" The man grabbed his wallet and pulled out a picture of his wife. "Here like this. It's my wife. This is what reality looks like." Picasso took the photograph, looked at it in his hand, smiled, and observed, "Really? She's very small - and flat too"

Modern Art, which was a great passion for Pablo Picasso was for Kai no more than a series of distortions.

Reality is a question of the thoughts which the observer has. Reality is in the eye of the beholder and thinker.

When combined with Consciousness, "Thought" comes to life. This story about Picasso and Kai shows that our experience of reality is individual for each person.

How I see my experience of the world and the universe depends on the thoughts going through my head and how Consciousness empowers my thoughts to become real to me.

We are not in control of where our Consciousness goes. It is just something that happens as we go through life. If we feel that we have a less than optimal life it doesn't mean that we've been focusing our Consciousness on something negative. This is very important.

We are not talking about mind control here. It is not our fault how our existence is created via Mind, Consciousness and Thought.

How you see your experience of the world and the universe, depends on the thoughts going through your head and how your Consciousness brings your thoughts to life. The Three Principles and mind control are totally different.

It's important not to misinterpret this point. The Three Principles have nothing to do with mind control. Mind control says that if we put our focus on what we want in our lives, then the things will magically appear. This is a technique.

The Three Principles is not a technique - something which you have to "do." Rather, it describes the reality of our human existence which is happening all the time whether we are aware of it or not. If we get an insight into this functioning, then we will get to see the simplicity of how it works.

## Different types of thoughts

Thought (in combination with Consciousness), is the function that creates images and perceptions in our brain. There are two distinct kinds of thoughts that have completely different qualities.

One kind of thought is conditioned thought. These are the thoughts we have picked up over our lifetimes.

The other kind of Thought is original and it is also absolutely clear and insightful. When we speak of "common sense" it is this type of Thought which we are referring to.

## Universal Thought and personal ego thought

"Thoughts suffer from an optical illusion of consciousness." Albert Einstein

It's extremely important to differentiate between personal thought and Thought with a capital T. By this I mean creative thoughts which flow through us and come to us when our mind is relaxed and is not overwhelmed by personal conditioned thoughts. Our quality of life depends on the kinds of thoughts that are enlivened with Consciousness. Our conditioned thoughts are the thoughts that we learn when we are growing up. They also have an important role to play.

## Let us look at an example

If you want your young daughter not to run across the street when cars are coming, then it's useful that she has conditioned thoughts. Conditioned thoughts are those thoughts that are learned through repetition.

Imagine your daughter is standing on the sidewalk (pavement – for my English readers) and she wants to cross the road. In this situation it is not good if she gets loads and loads of creative thoughts as to how she should cross the road.

It is more helpful if she remembers what her mum has taught her in her Highway Code Training.

## A mother is teaching her daughter to cross the road safely

Mother: "Stand at the side of the road.
Stop, look and listen out for any traffic.
Look right, look left, and look right again.
Then, if all is clear, walk quickly cross the road."

The result of this type of conditioned thinking is that your young daughter stays alive so that she can cross the road another day. Clearly, this is very helpful.

Sometimes though, these conditioned thoughts are not very useful. If, for example, as a child, your dad always told you that trying out new things is dangerous, then that's not helpful. As you grow up this aversion to risk might have a really negative effect on your life.

When our observations bypass these conditioned thoughts, we can see things with freshness and newness. These new creative insights are not based on past thinking or programmed thoughts that we've picked up from the past.

Our "universal" Thought has amazing power. It allows us to create wonderful paintings, such as in the works of Michelangelo and Leonardo da Vinci. We can design fantastic buildings and organize a delightful family picnic. Thoughts "with a capital T" provide us with a flow of creativity. Therefore, there are two types of thoughts that we are going to talk about here. These are personal thoughts and universal Thought.

## Universal Thought

It is the universal Thought that give us our ability to create. A universal Thought is the one that gives us the intuitive feeling that we should not go to visit this particular neighborhood in New York or Manchester. It might be dangerous to go there.

A universal Thought is the one that asks a question like - Shall I take this job, or shall I stay in my current position?

### The power of personal thoughts (with a small "t")

Personal, or ego thoughts are conditioned thoughts. Imagine walking around all the time with a set of headphones on but instead of listening to something enjoyable, you hear a voice in your head criticizing and complaining about every event which is going on in your life. That is the power of personal or ego or conditioned thoughts.

Michi (my dear girlfriend and partner) love Ireland. In Ireland, they have charming folklore centered around leprechauns. These little mythical guys are very difficult to see because they like to hide. They also have a bit of a bad reputation because they all too often get into mischief and like to trouble the unsuspecting.

Personal, ego or conditioned thoughts are a bit like these leprechauns. Consider a 'thought leprechaun' who might be shadowing you at every step of your life bringing continual worry and negativity. Whispering into your ear day and night with a voice of doom and gloom.

- *We should have left sooner. We are going to be late.*
- *You are driving too fast; you'll get another ticket.*
- *I am not going to pass my exams.*
- *Why not sell your house now?*
- *You'll never lose weight.*
- *I had that chocolate and I now feel ashamed of myself.*
- *Why on earth does it always rain on my birthday when I've got a party planned.*
- *And on and on and on.*

This constant voice might sound crazy to listen to. Nevertheless, it is a bit like what each of us is hearing a lot of the time. We have a running commentary going on in our heads that is commenting on all things which are happening. It is judging our actions and characterizing them in a negative light all the time.

So, where do all these personal thoughts and universal Thoughts and ego thoughts come from?

*"Your thoughts are like the artist's brush. They create a personal picture of the reality you live in."*

Sydney Banks

## The source of thoughts

As babies, we are born into the world as perfect beings. Babies have a spirit of adventure and an absence of judgment. A lot of adults grow out of this spirit of adventure. Our spirit of adventure fades. As young children grow up, they are continually learning and being given feedback that can either be supportive or damaging.

All too often, parents are blamed for any negative outcomes to do with their children. But it's not the parents' fault. Let's face it, children are confronted with a world where they are looked after by the big people who have a type of godlike omnipotent status. Babies and children are dependent.

## The mobile phone story

Let's imagine a mother who has not slept the night before and is exhausted. Now in a state of natural exploration into a fascinating new world, her two-year-old takes here brand new iPhone 18 mini and sticks it into the toaster. How does mum react? Smoke starts to come out of her ears, metaphorically, at least, and now comes the reaction!

**Oh, no! My brand new phone!**

"Get away from that and come and sit at the table," she commands, adding, "and never, ever, do that again!"

The small child doesn't really know what's going on but feels that whatever she has done was not a good idea. Subconsciously the toddler gets the message - playing with the stereo can be a really dangerous thing to do. So the toddler doesn't go there again. This situation might start to create a belief or a label that reads, "stereos are dangerous" or "it is best to always keep away from technical equipment." Twenty years later, that child, now an adult, might get a feeling of fear when their wife brings home a new stereo. That feeling of fear could be so intense that the husband now keeps away from technical stuff entirely.

## The source of thoughts

As babies, we are born into the world as perfect beings. Babies have a spirit of adventure and an absence of judgment. A lot of adults grow out of this spirit of adventure. Our spirit of adventure fades. As young children grow up, they are continually learning and being given feedback that can either be supportive or damaging.

All too often, parents are blamed for any negative outcomes to do with their children. But it's not the parents' fault. Let's face it, children are confronted with a world where they are looked after by the big people who have a type of godlike omnipotent status. Babies and children are dependent.

## Scratches on the window to our world

My dear girlfriend does not like dirty windows.

I don't either. The problem with dirt is that if there's enough of it, you can't see through the window. Scratches on glass are even worse than dirt. What I know now is that when we come to earth, we have a clear view of the world. Our experience often distorts our view so we can't see the world for what it truly is. Rather, we see it through the lens of our own preconceived and learned opinions. When we see how Mind, Consciousness, and Thought work then we have a different way of experiencing our lives.

## Serious stuff

How we think can have really serious consequences.

Let me illustrate this with a typical cowboy film. You have a situation in which two cowboys stand in front of one another to settle a dispute of some sort. The one who pulls his gun the slowest is the one who usually ends up either seriously injured or dead.

A more sophisticated version of this scenario is the classic dual which was the traditional way to solve disputes hundreds of years ago. Now consider the way we might resolve a dispute today. We might send a nasty email or text message. We might 'unfollow' the person who offended us on social media. Whether you consider the cowboy, the duel, or even the contemporary cutting off contact, it seems as though the behavior of the other person caused us to feel bad and caused our reactive behavior.

But is that really the case?

## What's really happening here? What is driving our behavior?

We often think that the reason we would behave in a certain way is because of the behavior of the other person. We have the belief that they "caused me" to react that way. Our thought processes happen so fast that we incorrectly presuppose that it's the behaviour of the other person which causes us to feel bad or to react.

**BEHAVIOUR leads to ACTION**

If this version of the situation were true we would need to ask why people react differently in the same situation.

For example, both Wendy and Jane could have had a terrible thing happen to them as a child – a comparably terrible thing.

Jane flourishes. She becomes a doctor and enjoys her life with her husband and family. Wendy, on the other hand, gets involved with the wrong crowd, becomes a drug addict and ends up living under a bridge.

They both experienced the same triggering event and yet their resultant behaviour was completely different – they were polar opposites. There must be something that causes the difference. There is- It is thought.

**BEHAVIOUR + THOUGHT leads to ACTION**

An event happens in our lives. Then we have a thought about what happened. And then we act or do not act on that thought. And there is more to consider.

With the Three Principles there is an additional element, namely, the element of Consciousness. When Consciousness gets mixed in with Thought, even though it's invisible, it provides the magical ingredient, the "secret sauce," which results in our thoughts appearing real to us.

**BEHAVIOUR + THOUGHT mixed with CONSCIOUSNESS leads to ACTION**

## The 1952 "PPenny"

Consider the fictitious, hypothetical case of the 1952 penny with two Ps embossed onto it – "**PP**enny." I love the story of the 1952 fictitious penny with the double P, which I heard about from Michael Singer. This story is intended to show how important our labels are and how they affect us.

**Just imagine this.**

You read an article in a newspaper which says that a very special penny minted in 1952 had two Ps on it. In other words, PPenny. Because of an error the double PP made the penny unique. Today that penny is worth more than £1 million.

Just imagine what happens to your heart rate when you find an old-looking penny in your pocket. You get excited. You check the date and find it was minted in 1952. And even more excitedly you can't quite read how the word penny is spelled. You hold your breath in anticipation as you get a cloth to wipe off the dirt from the word Penny.

Oh dear, it's only got one P. You just went from elation to disappointment.

The next day you read in the newspaper that a member of the Mafia issued a very, very serious threat against the person who finds this special penny – they will be killed. Murdered. They will be shot dead. So, what do you do? You hope that this now very dangerous penny with two Ps does not turn up in the loose change in your pocket. You check your coins. Thank goodness! I do not have one! You just went from fear to relief.

So, what's happening here?

The way we label a specific situation strongly affects the way we feel about it. When I have a thought that the PPenny is worth £1 million then I label this as very positive. When I have a thought that the Penny could

get me killed, then I label this as very negative. Our labels are directly linked to the kind of thoughts we have had. A positive thought can elicit a positive feeling.

## The Mind component

We can best describe Mind as the source of Thought and Consciousness. In fact, it is the source of absolutely everything. It provides the foundation for Thought and Consciousness.

Every experience we have as human beings is a result of our thoughts being injected with life, which we experience as our outside reality.

Mind provides the energy which every living being requires to survive and prosper. Our heart, for example, is not equipped with a Duracell battery. But it has the energy to continue pumping thousands and thousands of times. This energy must come from somewhere.

That 'somewhere' is Mind.

Although Mind is invisible, it provides the backdrop for everything that happens in our lives.

Although Mind is invisible, science has demonstrated that our universe is made up of an all-encompassing energy field. A sort of ocean of nothingness. Our whole universe is made up of matter, which is composed of materials, cells, atoms and on the minutest level, quarks and bosons. When these elements are observed, scientists see that they are separated by extremely large distances. They are separated by a "type of near-nothingness." In other words, there is nothing there apart from energy.

What we experience as matter, in the form of our bodies, for example, is an incredible creation that we experience as our outside world. This matter is made up of energy that oscillates at various frequencies. The different frequencies at which these waves oscillate determine which "matter" will result.

Human tissue, for example, would oscillate at a different frequency level from that of a piece of steel. Human beings have been imbued with the power and the special gift to experience our world in a way in which we can see, feel and touch it. However, all this is an incredible and unbelievably sophisticated illusion.

## The power of Consciousness

Imagine you are in your old dusty, neglected attic. It is dirty, dusty, dreary, and dark. You have your torch with you. You turn it on.

What you see will depend on which objects the light from your torch illuminates.

## The attic metaphor

Whether the light from your flashlight falls on a scary rat or beautiful silk rose does not affect the light. The light is neutral and just shines. The light, which could be viewed as a metaphor for inner essence can never be changed, affected, manipulated, or destroyed by anything at all in the outside world. The light is perfect and remains perfect. And always will continue to be perfect. It is the liveliness within us. That is what we are.

When I first heard about this Three Principles understanding I did not really understand a word. I just did not get the point. All I could see was that when people heard about it, and got an insight into it, they felt a lot better about themselves and their lives. Strange, I thought. I wanted to know what was happening to change the way people were feeling and experiencing their lives.

I was very curious. I had to answer a fundamental question for myself – What are the Three Principles? I had to define the Three Principles in simple terms for myself. So that is what I did and I'm sharing my answer here with you.

The Three Principles are a way of understanding how important our thinking is in our lives. Well, you might think; that's nothing new!

That's exactly what I thought. Loads of people have written about that.

As I learned about it though, I saw that the Three Principles went deeper than positive thinking. When I felt bad thoughts, I felt terrible. Sometimes, when I had better thoughts, I felt better. But I did not know what was behind this. The thinking and the feeling always went together.

However, I noticed that I only felt terrible when these thoughts became more active in my mind – when they seemed to take on a life of their own. This happened when my thoughts were being injected with Consciousness. I did do this. It was happening all the time to everybody. I wasn't thinking this way deliberately. It wasn't my fault, but I was feeling terrible.

## It wasn't my fault

It wasn't my fault that these thoughts were more "infused with life" than others. I didn't actually "do" anything to empower them.

Nobody empowers Consciousness. Consciousness is acting continually in our lives to make thought real to us.

When I spoke to people about my experience with these ideas, I found that they had a very similar experience.

## Consciousness – Aliveness

This "aliveness" was given a label by Sydney Banks. He called it Consciousness. I personally find this "aliveness" a truly incredible phenomenon! Adding this Consciousness to Thought creates life and a "realness" to our experience. This adding of Consciousness is not something which we do actively.

When we review my mum's experience at the rugby match, we saw how she first noticed the reality of her cold hands when Consciousness was added to Thought. Consciousness then is the component by which Thought comes alive.

## Mind – Oneness

The next principle was given the label "Mind" by Sydney Banks. What on earth is that? The only way I could understand this was by reviewing my own experience as a child. I sometimes had the experience in which I felt that I was part of something bigger than just my physical mass of bones, blood and skin. It was a sort of feeling of being one with everything.

I didn't know what this was at first. But I knew I had it. When I spoke to friends of mine, a lot of them said that they'd had the same feeling.

Maybe I was onto something here?

Slowly but surely, I started to get tiny insights into what was happening behind the scenes and how I was experiencing my life. This is what I understand as a feeling of "Oneness with the Universe."

This sounds very spiritual and in fact it is. In fact, many people who I have spoken to about the Three Principles understand this feeling and have experienced it personally for themselves. The fact that so many people have experienced this feeling of oneness makes 100% sense when we remember that the Three Principles are universal truths. They are in operation everywhere permanently. They affect all of us constantly as we go through our lives.

**Takeaway**

- ☑ BEHAVIOUR + THOUGHT mixed with CONSCIOUSNESS leads to ACTION
- ☑ The voice in your head cannot hurt you even though its effect on you feels so real
- ☑ She is a bit flat, isn't she (Picasso)

### CHAPTER 6

# Lessons Learned

*"We are spiritual beings living in a worldly experience."*

Sydney Banks

## The Basis of Spirituality

I'm not trying to evangelize or convince people one way or another. I can only really write about my own experience and my convictions. I can only share my journey from the darkness of depression into the light of a happier, more joyful life. As I mentioned, when I remember back to my days as a little boy I sometimes got the feeling of being part of something a lot bigger. I never understood what was going on, but it was a special feeling which came and went of its own accord. I never really thought about it very much - just an occasional, "Wow!

What was that feeling?"

But after a few years of experience I can now see that those feelings back then were mini-insights into the truths of our human experience here on earth. Wisdom was knocking at my door even as a child.

But I didn't really recognize it.

## Lesson 1 - Realising mental health

I "borrowed" this title from the book Realising Mental Health by Dr. Roger C. Mills who was a great pioneer in "The realizing Mental Health Movement.'

Dr. Mills writes, "Rethinking the nature of mental health we are beginning to see that mental health is more constant and more solid in human beings than mental illness. It also comes from inside out, not the other way round. Maybe a somewhat radical proposition to suggest that mental health is a core state of being for everyone, a natural state, to which people cannot lose access. Yet, perhaps more than anything, it has been most exciting for us to learn that mental health is much more than merely the absence of illness. It is, in and of itself, something that people can always get more of. They can deepen their well-being, their ability for creativity and insight, motivation, and productivity. When this happens, they enjoy their lives more than we had previously thought possible."

**Takeaway**

☑ Living a life according to the Three Principles is living a life aligned with a healthier mental state.

## Lesson 2 – Religion and modern science

I have sifted through some of the scientific literature which supports Sydney Bank's insights into Mind, Consciousness, and Thought. What I found particularly interesting was a conversation between Sydney Banks and Dr. George S. Pransky. I have written a summary of Dr. Pransky's comments on this conversation.

Here it is.

*"Syd said that many people from many different religions attended his talks and they all recognized that he was, in fact, talking about the core truth of their religion. In other words, Syd had received an insight into a truth that had been around for thousands and thousands of years.*

*It is fascinating too that when Sydney Banks taught scientists, they also were able to identify with the message of Mind, Consciousness, and Thought."*

**Takeaway**

☑ The Three Principles make sense on many different levels and in many spiritual and scientific contexts.

## Lesson 3 – Our sensory experience

*"Colourless, odorless, tasteless silence. Outside your brain, there is just energy and matter. Over millions of years of evolution, the human brain has become adept at turning this energy and matter into a rich sensory experience of being in the world."*

David Eagleman in The Brain - The Story of You

I love this quotation from the top scientist and author, David Eagleman. For me, it beautifully summarizes our human ability to experience reality.

## Lesson 4 – The source of all possibilities

One beautiful thing to remember about moving from your darkness into your light is that, by doing so, you open up a treasure chest of possibilities.

Anything can happen. Things can change and you can have new experiences. With new Thought, you can receive more creative ideas and these will lead you to taking new, fresh decisions. New actions will follow from these new decisions. The result is that these actions can then bring you in a completely new and different direction. This is when changes happen in your life.

Deepak Chopra expresses it well when he writes in his book Creating Affluence: The A-to-Z Steps to a Richer Life

*"A stands for all possibilities, absolute, authority, affluence, and abundance. The true nature of our ground state and that of the universe is that it is a field of all possibilities. In our most primordial form, we are a field of all possibilities. From this level, it is possible to create anything. This field is our own essential*

nature. It is our inner self. It is also called the absolute, and it is the ultimate authority. It is intrinsically affluent because it gives rise to the infinite diversity and abundance of the universe...Behind the visible garment of the universe, beyond the mirage of molecules, the maya — or illusion — of physicality, lies an inherently invisible, seamless matrix made up of a nothingness. This invisible nothingness silently orchestrates, instructs, guides, governs, and compels nature to express itself with infinite creativity, infinite abundance, and unfaltering exactitude into myriads of designs and patterns and forms."

Living a life according to the Three Principles is living a life of abundance. This does not necessarily refer to material abundance. There are other types of abundance. For example, we can have an abundance of friends or enjoyable and nice ways to spend our time doing the things we love. Travelling, playing or creating music are other examples.

## Lesson 5 - Dealing with our stuff

One day I was listening to Michael Singer, a wonderful speaker and bestselling author. I was listening to him in my car and I finally understood something important. He was talking about how we collect old stuff as we go through life.

Life happens. Things occur which might not be so good. Things also sometimes happen which are wonderful. We collect old thoughts, and they remain in our minds. They stay there. Stuck. Not leaving - a bit like unwanted visitors. This sometimes creates a problem. The problem is not the thoughts themselves. The real problems occur when they take up our attention.

Living a life according to the Three Principles is being aware that thoughts come and go through our minds constantly.

When we remember that our thoughts are always changing, then we can be more relaxed when we have bad feelings. Because we know that thoughts and feelings go together, we can be sure that when our thinking changes, which it always does, then so will our feelings.

## Lesson 6 - Spiritual insights

I strongly feel that The Three Principles also very much apply to the spiritual area of our lives. In my view, the Three Principles help to bring together all the great ancient masters' spiritual insights which they have had received over history.

Contemporary masters have also guided humanity towards an understanding of life and the universe based on the spiritual conviction of what existence and life are.

It's fascinating to see how all these spiritual pioneers helped their followers find the truth. In the same way, the great masters of the past and present have pointed to looking inside ourselves for the answers to the really important questions of life. It is there, when we go inside, that we will find the answers to the questions which we are looking for.

The three world religions, Christianity, Islam, and Judaism talk about - nothing being separate, and everything being interconnected.

I found it fascinating to discover that the leaders of these religions all came up with the same or a very similar conclusion.

Time after time great insights showed the reality of what the universe is - an unimaginably giant oneness, which can be experienced by us as human beings via our senses.

If we can slow down enough, we might be given the grace of insight which will open up a completely new world to us. Our continual internal chatter can distract us from the oneness and wholeness and feeling of unity that most people are striving for. When we get quiet enough and allow this inner chatter to fade away, we can experience more of our real nature. Striving to see something in the world out there is the wrong place to look.

The religions of the world are continually reminding us to look inside. There you will find the answer to what you're looking for.

## Jesus

*The truth will set you free"*

John 8:32

I am going to relate my own understanding of the Three Principles to what Jesus preached. I believe that the Three Principles are in line with many of the things which Jesus talked about in his sermons.

The kingdom is within you - This means that you don't have to do anything. We all have within us the ability to achieve inner peace.

You must die to be reborn - But clearly, this doesn't mean the death of our physical bodies.

But what does it mean?

The "you" here refers to our fearful personal ego-self which wants to hold onto its power at all costs. We just need to see how this personal ego-self is not really who we are. It is the result of our upbringing and our learning in the past.

These are just two examples from the biblical scriptures which reaffirm that the Three Principles and how they help us to see our true nature.

## Indian Traditions

In a fascinating discussion over dinner, in Spain, a friend explained to me the way in which the Veda says exactly what the Three Principles are pointing towards. She quoted the Shiv Shakti. "It is the male and female energies of the universe coming together. Form and formless come together - and there is the miracle of creation!"

The other world religions including Judaism, Buddhism, Hinduism, Islam all contain elements of the Three Principles in their narrative of faith and belief.

**Takeaway**

☑ Living a life according to the Three Principles is compatible with the world's greatest spiritual thinkers, guides, and religions.

## Lesson 7 - Contemporary Masters

The Three Principles are not only supported by spiritual and religious teachings. They are also supported by the works of many of the world's greatest thinkers who demonstrated aspects of this understanding. They reveal the same truth.

## Albert Einstein

I am personally not a lover of political-type language. I cannot stand listening to empty comments without any concrete research findings or scientific evidence to back them up.

That's why I enjoy contemplating Albert Einstein's descriptions of how the universe is constructed. Einstein and other great scientists have proven the reality of "phenomena" such as a spiritual understanding which have been the basis of our human civilization's spiritual understanding for thousands of years.

Albert Einstein proved that everything that we can see is a form of energy that is vibrating at different frequencies. This means that although our physical senses cannot feel these vibrations, they are nevertheless always there.

A table, for example, has a different frequency to a tablecloth. But these objects are still energy that is vibrating at different frequencies.

We can use the example of electricity. Let us imagine we are trying to get an electric mixer to work. We might focus a hundred percent of our energy on the physical parts of the mixer. It might be, however, that we are on the wrong track and the actual problem is that the invisible power – the electricity - coming through the electric cable, is not getting through to the mixer. The energy is not reaching the mixer.

In my view, this section is really important so please stay with me for a moment to learn from this innovative thinker's words which echo the Three Principles. Michael Singer says we are the Consciousness looking at and observing the sum of our learned experiences. Observing is the key word here. If we can observe our learned experiences, then we cannot be those learned experiences. The two are separate.

Singer challenged thinkers like Skinner who said that our existence is only based on our learned experiences. In other words, Skinner believed that our experience is our learned experience and nothing else.

With Skinner, there is no room for any spiritual essence or Consciousness. Skinner believed that we are not the observer viewing our experience from outside. If this were true, said Michael Singer, it would mean that we would be locked in a mental box forever. We would have no way of knowing how our experience of life really works. We would not be conscious of what is happening. But this is not true.

If it were true, then it would be a truly hopeless situation. Singer provides us with the hope that we are not imprisoned by our past human experiences. We have the incredible gift of being conscious. Our higher self can observe our personal ego or self. So although our personal or ego-self often gets us into, the truth is that we are not this personal ego-self. Our "ego-self" is not who we really are. We are the one, the consciousness who is watching our human, personal or ego-self. Singer's key insight is that we are the Consciousness. We are looking at and observing the sum of our learned experiences.

Michael Singer's statement is in line with everything we've been discussing in this book so far and all the masters of the past. They have been pointing to these truths over the whole of human history.

## Anthony de Mello

Anthony de Mello was a Jesuit priest who had a few differences of opinion with the papacy. However, he did not allow the papacy to silence him in speaking the truth.

In his wonderful book titled Awareness, he explained a four-step process to wisdom. This is described as a system. There is no system to gaining insight into the Three Principles understanding. However, there are some close similarities between Anthony De Mello's teaching and The Three Principles vision of the truth.

De Mello's Model actually has four steps, and we are going to look at just two of these steps here:

**Step one** - Get in touch with your negative emotions. Do not try to change negative feelings.

Just allow them to be. If we do not try to change these negative feelings, then we relieve the pressure on us to change. Paradoxically, this letting go of trying actually allows us to change more easily because our negative thoughts and feelings can pass through our minds and leave us more easily.

**Step two** - These negative feelings are in you, not in reality outside. So, stop trying to change reality. Stop trying to think of people as the cause of your misery. We spend lots and lots of time trying to change our outside circumstances, our job, our romantic partner, our car, our kids, the color of the walls in our house, how young or how old we look, and so on. But these are not where the answers lie.

Never identify with that feeling. Do not take it too seriously. It is not you. It has nothing to do with your true self. Anthony De Mello refers to the true self as "I." In other words, you are not the feeling even though these feelings seem to be so real. But they are not you. Your feelings will naturally change as your thoughts change.

"No event on earth has the power to disturb you or hurt you. No event, condition, situation, or person. Nobody told you this; they told you the opposite."

Tony De Mello

**Takeaway**

☑ Living by the Three Principles unites us with some of the greatest minds whose writings were closely aligned with the Three Principles. The truth of the Three Principles has underscored the truths of the great masters who have come before us.

**Resource**

Awareness by Anthony de Mello
This is a wonderful spiritual book and is worth contemplating on and re-reading.

## Lesson 8 - Life and death

*"If the thermometer had read a degree or two less, I would have frozen to death."*
Mark Twain

The freezer and the power of thought is a story reported by David Mikkelson and it illustrates the power of thought. It is sadly not a joke.

A man finds himself locked in a walk-in freezer. He is convinced he will die and begins writing letters. His letters end with a final passage where he is saying that he cannot write anymore because his fingers are beginning to freeze. When they find him dead not only do they find the letters but they discover that the freezer's temperature never dropped below 50 degrees. The man wasn't "really objectively cold." He had "thought himself to death." This short and simple story underlines the power of thought.

It shows the way in which our experience of life is affected by how our Thought and Consciousness combine. It is this mixture of these powerful invisible elements (Thought and Consciousness) which creates our reality.

## Lesson 9 – Feeling Compassion

When people act with compassion, this behavior is a direct result of people having compassionate thoughts. When people act with hate, this behavior comes as a result of hateful thoughts. A compassionate way of being is the natural beautiful state of little children.

My reference to hatred and hateful thoughts leads us directly to the question - why do people behave in a hateful way towards each other?

In the worst case this hatred turns into killing.

## Why do people kill each other?

I have never personally met a person who has killed another person. But I know somebody who has. She works in the prison system. In talking about those who have killed, she explained that many wished that they could go back in time and undo their act of killing. Maybe if they had seen how powerful our thinking is they would have acted differently. If they had seen how our thinking is transformed into unbelievably strong feelings, they might have stopped to think before acting. They might have been able to get some clarity and perspective on what they were about to do.

I only know that I personally am very grateful that I did not have access to a knife when I have been in an almighty rage due to some conflict between my thinking, or values, and those of another person.

The same can be said of war. It is horrifying to write this, but it is the truth. War has the same origin – it begins with a thought. But in this case those people who have great political power (and have horrible inhuman thoughts) tragically affect the destiny of millions and millions of people.

☑ Living by the Three Principles unites us with some of the greatest minds whose writings were closely aligned with the Three Principles. The truth of the Three Principles has underscored the truths of the great masters who have come before us.

☑ The Three Principles offer a clear understanding of how we function as people and this understanding can encourage compassion towards others and reduce the risk of war, conflict, and pain.

**War**

The tragic unfolding of events in Ukraine show how the thoughts of one man when given unlimited power can affect the lives of millions of people.

**Lesson 10 - Returning to our true state.**

This is the true story of Angela, a medical doctor in Emilia-Romagna who supports children with psychiatric challenges. The story is about a magical conversation she had with Alessio, her little boy, when he was 3.

He called a little child to him and placed the child among them. And he said: *"Truly, I tell you unless you change and become like little children, you shall not enter the kingdom of heaven"*

Matthew 18:2-4

Angela uses the Three Principles to help her children to experience how powerful they really are, as people – how innately wise. She demonstrates the wisdom of children through this anecdote about her son, Alessio and what he taught her when he was three years old.

Angela:   One day when I came home Alessio had broken several objects – he was at that stage of breaking things. So, I asked him what he was doing. I pointed out that he was doing things that weren't very good. He was breaking his toys. Making a mess. And I asked him to stop.

He started to cry and then he said:

Alessio:   Listen, mummy... You have to tell me that I'm perfect.

Angela:   I told him he was perfect - a beautiful boy. But breaking his toys was not a good thing to do!

But he persisted and kept insisting that I don't say he was bad – he suggested I say that he was just doing something 'not so good.'

I then asked him how I could teach him the right things?

Angela:   How can I say stop doing something wrong! How can I teach you the right things?

Alessio was firm. He only wanted to hear from me that he was perfect and that his mummy loved him.

As it turned out, my son didn't want to be defined by his actions – he wanted to hear an expression of love. His inner essence is good. This is what he wanted to hear.

When I spoke to Alessio about these things I think I learned about little children.

Angela was very generous to share this true story with me and she said that she was happy for me to share it here.

**Takeaway**

☑ If you live by the Three Principles you will have the humility to see how much we can learn from little children.

## Lesson 11 - Films as metaphors

This whole book promises that the Three Principles provide an understanding of how our experience of life works. This idea appears in many different places in our normal lives.

It even appears in classic films which have a very wide audience.

In this section I'm going to be looking at two films, The Matrix, and A Beautiful Mind. I will examine how the Three Principles are reflected in the experiences of some of the characters in these movies.

### The Matrix

In The Matrix, the basic premise of the film is the idea that the life which people are living in is not real. Furthermore, the film is suggesting that there is no objective reality.

As we watch The Matrix, which is actually science fiction movie viewed from a philosophical perspective, we are continually being asked the important question, namely;

**What is real?**

The film portrays an idea of life as an elaborately reconstructed experiment - an experiment that has been set up and designed by machines. The people in the matrix are mere players. The entire core of The Matrix focuses on the fact that we are living in an illusion - that the entire fabric of our day-to-day life is an illusion.

One of the characters, Morpheus explains that the matrix is a computer-generated dreamworld built to keep the characters under control, so they can serve as an energy source to continue to power their machines.

The critical metaphor of the film is that we simply have no way of knowing what is real because we are not able to experience any objective reality. With the Three Principles, as in the Matrix, we are able to see what is really happening in the background. We can see that our reality is being generated via our thoughts and that this insight allows us to see the world differently.

**A Beautiful Mind**

The film A Beautiful Mind tells the saga of the mathematician John Nash. He is brilliantly portrayed by Russell Crowe. The film shows the journey from his early days as a student at Princeton to his ultimate triumph over his mental illness and his subsequent winning of the Nobel Prize.

We see how Nash and his roommate at Princeton develop a very strong friendship that lasts beyond their graduation. We also meet a dubious FBI agent who recruits Nash to help decipher complicated war codes. His roommate eventually returns with his lovely young niece. Nash finds her very charming. Then suddenly, Nash has a breakdown and we, the audience, discover that the roommate, the FBI agent, and the little girl are simply figments of Nash's imagination. They don't exist at all. They never did exist, no matter how real they appeared to Nash.

I love the end of the film.

John Nash, now on medication, knows that the little girl is an illusion and because he has had an insight about this, he does not let it bother him any longer. He just ignores the illusion even though he still sees the child (in the background) while he is going about his normal life.

It was John Nash's final acceptance that these life-like apparitions were representations of his subconscious that allowed him to be able to see that they had no power over him. He could not only cope but also enjoy his life.

When we get an insight into how our experience is being created inside our minds via thinking, then our experience does not frighten us anymore. Nash is a wonderful example of how we can experience our lives by seeing through what appears to be happening.

When we fully realize that our thoughts cannot hurt us, and can be allowed to pass through our minds, then we are finally free.

**Takeaway**

- ☑ A Beautiful Mind is a beautiful movie
- ☑ Be in the present moment as much as possible
- ☑ We are spiritual being living a human experience Sydney Banks
- ☑ Just as the Three Principles show, we all see images. But it is just that the visions we see are inside our beautiful minds, and not "outside," as they were for John Nash.

**Resource**

Film - A Beautiful Mind

**Question for reflection**

What can little children teach us about life which we as adults, tend to forget?

### CHAPTER 7

# How the Three Principles Help

*"We all live in our own thought-created reality. If we don't think something, it does not enter our reality. It doesn't matter if it's "there" or not. The only reality we can see and experience is the reality we create via our own thinking."*

Quotation by Sydney Banks as shred by Judith Sedgeman.

## Three short case studies

In this chapter, I am going take you through **three case studies**. They are about Jack, Justin, and John.

After that, you will read about **eleven ways** in which the Three Principles can give us a completely different way of looking at everyday situations and challenges.

## The 11 topics are:

1. Presenting
2. Meetings
3. Relationships
4. Moods
5. Confidence
6. Stress
7. Money
8. Fear and insecurity
9. Avoiding suicide
10. Coaching
11. Learning and optimism

I'm going to begin this chapter with the three short case studies.

We all have insights into many things in life, even though we might not describe them as insights. Some people call them thoughts out of the blue. Others call them common sense, while others might call them wisdom.

Here are three people who demonstrate how insights helped them to see things differently.

### Case study 1 - Jack in the pool

Empathy is having compassion for others. This is a major component of the Three Principles.

Consider this example of Jack in the pool.

Jack loves swimming and he tells a great story of how quickly our levels of understanding or consciousness can change. I recall how Jack told us the story of his afternoon swimming session. He was doing lengths in the pool, quietly minding his own business. Then some kids arrived. They splashed about, often blocking his path, as he tried to complete his laps.

"Why don't these kids go and mess around somewhere else," he thought as he became increasingly annoyed and irritated. Then he had a flash of insight.

Maybe they don't realize they are in my way. Maybe they are just focused on having fun. After all, he had also bumped into people before without realizing it. His mood changed. It started to go up.

Another thought popped into his mind - maybe their parents never told them to be aware of their surroundings or watch out for others. Or worse, what if their parents treated them badly or ignored them?

His irritation melted away and a positive feeling of compassion flooded over him.

Although our thoughts come arbitrarily, and we cannot control the thoughts which come into our minds, we can decide whether to allow unhelpful thoughts to pass by us. We can just let them go.

## Case study 2 – The brand-new cello

Justin's daughter had a little cello that she enjoyed playing. One day it was time to say goodbye to her small, beloved child-sized cello.

She was going to get a bigger one. This sounds like great news, doesn't it? Well, even though she was graduating to a full-sized instrument, she still held on tight to her much-treasured little cello. She would not let it go. She even hid behind the sofa wrapping her arms around it. She also refused to get into the car to go to the music store.

Justin was beginning to get a bit frustrated by his daughter's behavior. But he saw how important that little cello was to her.

Then, a wonderful question popped into his mind. He asked his daughter a great question, "Would it be okay for you if we took a photo of your cello before we take it back in exchange for your brand new one?"

She smiled lovingly and nodded with approval. He handed over his iPhone and she took the picture. Then she happily got into the car and they went on their way together to buy her full-sized, brand new, shiny cello.

## Case study 3 - I had a very old teddy bear

I had a very old teddy bear that was about to get thrown away because it was disgustingly dirty and irreparably damaged. But it was still my beloved Teddy. I decided to take a photo before it was thrown out. Now, years later, even though Teddy is no longer "alive," every time I look at (or think of) the picture the same loving feelings flood back.

## Feeling different starts inside

We often think that our experience of "things out there" comes from the objects themselves. But as we all know this can't be true. It is just pure common sense that a feeling can't travel from a teddy bear and get into my body. Feeling differently has nothing to do with what we have. It's about acknowledging that our experience of the world comes from inside us.

## 11 ways the Three Principles help in everyday situations

In the final section of this book, I'm going to look at eleven typical situations which people often struggle with. You will read about the insights that helped them and me to see things from a different perspective. Let me start with presenting.

**The 11 topics are:**

1. Presenting
2. Meetings
3. Relationships
4. Moods
5. Confidence
6. Stress
7. Money
8. Fear and insecurity
9. Avoiding suicide
10. Help with coaching, training and consulting
11. Help with Learning


## 1. Presenting

I am always amazed at how well people can speak spontaneously. I had a very dear uncle, my uncle Roy, who was particularly good at this. He was so captivating to listen to.

I always wondered how it was that presenters like my uncle were so good at it. They come across as being so authentic and as truly speaking from the heart.

Practically everyone can do this in social situations. They can tell great anecdotes, jokes and are calm and relaxed.

When they stand up to speak to a group often their natural confidence goes out of the window.

## Why is this?

By the end of this section, you will be able to answer this question.

So, why are some people so good at public speaking?

Being in the moment – Then, I thought about myself when I'm in any situation where I have to make a presentation. I noticed something very helpful.

I realized that when I am not thinking about what I am going to say, I speak the best. This allows me to be in the moment. This is what author Eckhart Tolle talks about when he refers to accessing the power of now.

Preparation - Does it make sense to prepare your talk? Yes, it does. But the point is not to try to remember what you want to say word for word. Instead, just practice and then forget about it. When you speak, allow new, fresh thoughts to guide you as to what you want to say. Allow yourself to go with the flow.

This is how the Three Principles teacher, Dr. George S. Pransky, described how he handles his thoughts.

## Dr. Pransky and his client - a short dialogue

One of his clients is asking George about his strategy when he presents. He asks...

Client:   What do you do, George, when you get distracted by your own personal thinking.
Don't you get nervous?

George:  Yes, I do

Client:   What do you do about it?

George:  Well, I know that they are just thoughts and they almost always come and go if I just allow that to happen. So, I don't actually do anything. The less I do, the better.

Client:   What if your crazy thoughts do not leave for your whole one-hour talk.

George:  If I understand what is happening, then I know that they will go away all by themselves.

Client:   What if they don't go away?

George:  Well, then they don't go away but that is OK too. I just continue to feel nervous until they eventually go away. Thoughts are continually changing so it is not possible for them to remain in one spot for any great length of time. That's not unless you hold them in your attention by focusing on these "crazy" thoughts.

Paradoxically, if I try to make them go away, the focus I put on these worrying thoughts, will make them stay even longer.

Because I know the nature of thought and I know they will go sooner or later, then it does not make sense to try to force them to leave.

This then is the nature of human thought. Thoughts are dynamic and they are constantly changing.

Any sort of public speaking brings up the question: Why are some people interesting and some unbelievably boring?

I believe that boring speakers talk from memory or they just read their notes. This causes them to have no connection with their audience. Without any connection it is impossible to inspire people. Inspiration is transported not only via the content but also by the charisma and personality of the speaker.

**The story of George's two uncles**

George tells the story of two types of uncles - the boring type and the spontaneous type. The boring uncle always spoke as if he were reading from a script. He was bored to death with his own life. And as a result, he gave "nothing of himself" to his audience. His heart was just not in it. So, he bored his audience to death. A bored person comes across to her/his audience as boring.

On the other hand, the interesting uncle was a pleasure to be with. He clearly enjoyed his life. New ideas kept popping into his mind like cafeteria trays that just pop up naturally and spontaneously. It was a pleasure to talk to him.

Personally, when I plan to speak, I prepare not so that I can recite my talk by reading off the words like an actor might recite her lines. Rather than doing this, when I am ready to speak I put my preparation away and speak spontaneously. My preparation raises my confidence. When I have prepared well, I can talk with a spirit of enjoyment. When I'm in the flow, it's almost as if I don't have any thoughts. I don't analyse what I am saying or how I'm saying it. I simply speak and enjoy the process.

## Summary

As people we are wired to speak naturally.

However, personal thoughts of fear and insecurity often muddy the waters and impede our natural speaking ability. When a question like, "How am I doing?" pops into our heads, it is just not helpful.

If our thoughts look real and serious, they are a problem – we give them too much attention.

If they look like thoughts, they are not a problem.

When we do not give them attention and they float past our minds like clouds in the sky. This allows space for fresh, new thoughts to appear.

It is not a problem if you feel insecure. What is important, though, is your relationship to your thinking in the moment. Feeling insecure and having insecure thoughts is really not a problem. What is a problem is taking these insecure thoughts seriously?

A struggling public speaker comes from a position of, "I am in trouble here. I am useless at public speaking." This makes the speaker tight, nervous, and boringly predictable. Any great public speaker comes from a position of "My thoughts (maybe even negative thoughts) will just come and go and I'm just going to allow them to move on by themselves."

Not taking very much notice of your incoming thoughts is a performance enhancer, whatever you are trying to achieve.

This insight gives great speakers a free mind so that they can speak authentically and charismatically.

**Takeaway**

☑  Paradoxically, thinking too much when you give a talk limits the quality and depth of your presenting.

## 2. Help with Meetings

I personally used to be distracted almost a hundred percent of the time. And this was not only in meetings. I was so tied up in my own personal thoughts that I couldn't really focus on other people.

This still sometimes happens to me. But the difference is that I now know that these thoughts will go away. Thoughts come and go.

People know when you're not really with them in a meeting. They know when you're not really listening. Very often people think about what they want to say when the person has finished.

I was good at playing a role in meetings and occasionally people didn't notice that my thoughts were elsewhere. But I experienced the meetings as stressful, hard work, and not very enjoyable.

What is the secret to a good, high-performance meeting? What has to happen in peoples' minds to be able to have great meetings? And what determines whether a meeting is unsuccessful? The quality of the thinking that goes on in a meeting determines how effective the meeting is going to be.

New, creative thought is what we are looking for in a meeting. This is not a rehash of all the ideas which you have talked about a hundred times before. If you are just repeating ideas that have already been discussed, then there is no reason to have a meeting at all. You might as well just send out the minutes of a previous meeting or write an executive summary of the ideas.

Lots of money is at stake in decisions that are made in boardrooms around the world. There are many reasons to have a meeting, but the most exciting and potentially productive reason to have a meeting is to create transformation. So, a key question to ask is;

Does this meeting produce new ideas and new thinking?

Many people think that this list of characteristics below represents the key success factors for a great meeting.

- An agenda
- Knowledgeable attendees
- Smart attendees
- Lots of experience
- Lots of background on the topic

However, these elements or qualities actually have little correlation with new ideas. Quality of new ideas and quality of results is the key to great meetings. The quality of new ideas in the meeting is one hundred percent connected with the quality of the thinking that people experience in the meeting. Also, the quality of the results of the meeting is directly related to the quality of the thinking that goes on in the minds of the participants.

This might sound like a radical idea. And it is.

It goes against many of the latest ideas on how executives should lead great meetings. But just think of those people who have changed the world with their thinking.

Albert Einstein's thoughts were extremely creative. As a child, he didn't do so well at school. However, he imagined himself riding on a beam of light and came up with his famous theory of relativity.

Walt Disney too was able to imagine something inconceivable to people at the time. The incredible Walt Disney theme park is a magical place that people visit from all over the world.

People do not think well when they are dispirited. That's why optimism is so important. Of course, optimism is not objective. It is totally subjective and originates inside our minds.

The advantage of optimism is that it helps people enter a positive state of mind so that they can generate new and creative ideas that can inspire change.

The state of peoples' minds when they are in meetings is the key to the result which they will get at the end.

When people are bummed out, overstressed, worried and nervous about making mistakes then they are not going to be relaxed.

Under these conditions, new thoughts and ideas often get blocked.


**Where do great ideas come from?**

Where great ideas come from is no great mystery.

We know that great ideas come when we are taking a shower, enjoying a drive in the countryside, or just sitting in our favorite armchair and daydreaming.


What do these situations have in common?

They are not threatening. we are relaxed and not trying to do anything specific, ideas just come to us. And we say that they just come "out of the blue." It is almost as if they fall out of the sky as a gift or reward for not trying too hard.

This goes against the whole idea of what many people understand by an effective thought process.

Normally, people talk about goal setting and setting stressful timelines. However, sometimes this method of trying to achieve goals is counterproductive.

Goal setting is important, but it depends on how you set your goals in the first place. So, you need to have a positive outlook on planning. Sometimes, goals need to be revised as you go along in a project, so you need a positive outlook on change. The key point is that you need to be flexible.

George Pransky often used to attend meetings in companies to see how they were doing and what tone the meetings were being held in.

After visiting one company, in particular, he later reflected on the effectiveness of the meeting.

He said that sometimes he thought, "If I had a month to live, then one place I would not want to be is in this meeting." The participants seemed not to be enjoying the meeting. They were bogged down. They were negative. They didn't appear to like each other. And the company was not doing very well at all. Later, not surprisingly, it went bankrupt.

Take a break during the meeting. This often helps to change the state of the participants. Their internal feeling state is the key.

When the meeting starts, and it feels like everyone is struggling as though they are wading through thick syrup, then it's time for a break. It is time to get some fresh air.

Go and have a cup of coffee. If you are British, make a cup of tea and enjoy a digestive biscuit with your tea.

Do anything just to change the negative internal feeling that the participants are displaying.

Humor is an excellent antidote to negativity. It is very difficult for people to be in a negative state if they are smiling or laughing.

When we begin to understand where ideas come from, namely from our own relaxed and open state, then we can take responsibility for the efficiency and results of the meeting. This does not need to be done in a stressful way. It needs to be done in a way that allows the kind of thinking that encourages creative ideas. However, if participants think discouraging thoughts, they are going to have discouraging feelings. If we think positive thoughts, we can invite in positive feelings. Feeling and thinking are two sides of the same coin. They are inextricably connected. People often think that our feelings come from what happens outside, in the world. But it doesn't work like that.

## The key

What happens in the world is an event and we attach thoughts to that event. Then we get a feeling which is a direct result of the type of thought that we are having. This process is at work all the time, below the surface, behind the curtain of our lives. We often don't realize that this is happening. This is how life works.

And this understanding explains why some people who have an objectively very difficult life (for example, not much money, poor health, family tragedy) can still be in a good state or mind. They are happy despite their difficult outer experiences. That's because they always see the best in life rather than looking at the negative aspects. Their thinking is positive and so their feelings are positive too. Of course, it works the other way round too.

We all know people who, on the outside have an incredible life. They are rich, have a beautiful wife, wonderful kids, a great house, and maybe even a bright red Lamborghini. They could be world-famous actors or influencers with millions of fans on their social media feeds. And then one day we read that they were found in their luxury flat hanging from the ceiling – the result of another tragic suicide.

This example shows just how important our thinking is. Our thinking affects how we feel and how we feel has a direct effect on how we act and what we do in the world.

When our minds are free, we have greater access to the source of new and creative thoughts. Some people might call this source, universal intelligence. An example of this intelligence is the ability of salmon to find its way back to its breeding ground. Another example is how a foetus develops into a baby, then a toddler, then a young child, teenager, and adult.

### Where on earth do great ideas come from?

Have you ever said this to yourself? I never knew I could ever think that! We sometimes surprise ourselves with our own brilliance. But our great ideas come from a source that is totally different from the repetitive thinking which comes from our ego-mind.

Some call these ideas wisdom. Others might call them moments of genius or intuition. My dad called it common sense. The important thing is that they come from a special source and have a completely different quality to the thinking which happens when we are trying to think in a stressful constrained way.

## A thinking survey – Nothing on my mind

Dr. George Pransky and his research team asked 150 people in San Francisco this question – When do you get your very best thoughts?"

Here are some of the answers they got back.

- When I am on vacation.
- When I am in the shower.
- When I'm driving.
- I can think of others like…
- When I'm playing with my kids.
- When I'm doing something which I love.
- When I'm looking at the sunset.
- When I am taking my dog for a walk.

The researchers then asked – "So, what do these situations have in common?" The answer is that they are all situations when people had a free mind. They had nothing on their minds. It is really funny (or sad, depending on how you look at it) that managers spend fifty weeks trying to generate new ideas at work. Then they go on holiday for two weeks and they get more ideas during those two weeks than they had during the entire year at work. That's how powerful it is to be in a state where your mind can be free. What then do we need to create new thoughts? We need an environment that supports the following:

- A light atmosphere
- A warm tone
- A reflective, non-threatening atmosphere
- A lively approach
- A relaxed ambience
- When people are on a retreat
- A location away from the office
- Personal interaction

Very often what happens is that someone will bring up an idea and the next thing that happens is that another person will say, "I disagree with that. I think that's a bad idea."

This has massive ramifications on the results of the meeting. New creative ideas need to be thought of sensitive butterflies that have just been born. They are like a new-born baby - vulnerable and in need of nurturing.

Newly born butterflies are fragile and if they are neglected or mistreated, they just die. It is the same with ideas. However, if colleagues in the meeting have a receptive attitude and are open to finding merit in any ideas that are proposed, then these ideas can stand on their own.

It might be then, that some people disagree with the idea. But at least that newly formed idea has had the opportunity to be heard and to be taken seriously. The key to getting lots of great ideas is to have lots of ideas

A great atmosphere in any meeting is when the participants come up with a lot of new ideas in a playful and creative way. It is great to get lots of ideas that are not censored.

This is a recipe for great results as well as happy employees who enjoy contributing to the health of the organization.

**Takeaway**

☑ The state of peoples' minds when they are in meetings is the key to the result which they will get at the end.

## 3.  Relationships

*"I've worked on my relationship for years – it seems to
me. The harder I work on it the more flaws I do see.
It is when I weary of the working – and give up – that's when I
know, All the joys of being with him. And the feelings grow and
grow."*

**From Coming Home by Sue Pettit**


Let me begin this section with a crazy question.

If, as a marriage counsellor, you wanted to make sure your new
clients, who were having a problem with their relationship, split
up or continue to have fights, what would be your first
question? Consider this opening question in a counselling
session.

Marriage counsellor: "Please list all the problems you are having
at the moment. Then we can go through them and knocked
them off one problem at a time."

Why is this approach such a relationship killer? Because it takes
people back into the past.

Both parties begin to think about all the negative things that
happened in the client's relationship. Because thought and
feelings are linked, this mad method results in the client getting
bad feelings about their partner. This is a terrible start if we
want to feel positive towards our spouse or loved one.

This reminds me of a story that Sydney Banks shared about a
course he attended.

The participants had signed up for the course because they were having conflicts at home. The first exercise which the teacher asked them to do was to turn to the person next to them and have an argument with them!

How on earth are you going to teach people to be kinder to each other if the first thing you teach them is how to argue with their partner.

For Sydney Banks, this just did not make any sense. It was just not logical.

So, now, back to our "marriage counsellor."
What exactly is the effect of his question?

"Please list all the problems…"

This question takes the clients in a direction where they move into a very low mood. In a low mood it's practically impossible to come up with any creative solutions. Everything looks black and we tend to see problems as impossible to solve. The glass really seems half-empty. What might normally seem to be a soluble problem has now become an insoluble challenge.

The counsellor might then say that it seems as if some deep-seated problems need to be worked on. It is going to take ages, he says, and will require lots and lots of work to get back on track. By now the client, who has come for help,

(If we could really call this "help") is visualizing a horror scenario of exercises, new conflictual arguments, and eventual divorce.

Clearly, we need a completely different approach.

It's important that the partners really understand how important moods are in relationships.

Everybody has good and bad moods or high and low moods. When we are in a low mood it's best not to try to make any life-changing decisions such as these.

Who do you want to marry?
Do you want to buy a house together?
Do you want to get a divorce?
Before you even think of answering these life-changing questions, then please wait for a more positive mood.

"In a healthy state, we are like Dr. Jekyll. When we lose this state, "hello Mr. Hyde!"

Dr. and Mrs. Jekyll always have a good marriage. Mr. and Mrs. Hyde always have problems.

It takes only one Mr. Jekyll to move a marriage towards health, love and a much happier future"

In other words, it only takes one Dr. Jekyll to ask his or her partner to join him in a dance.

**Takeaway**

☑ Marriage counsellor: "Please list all the problems you are having at the moment. Then we can go through them and knock them off one problem at a time."

☑ Why is this "list the problems approach" a gigantic relationship killer? Because it takes people back into the past.

## 4.  Help with bad moods

I had the pleasure of being taught by Dr. George Pransky. I remember one session particularly well.

I was in a bad mood. Some people would say I was very depressed. I couldn't shake off this low mood. George said something extremely important to me which I will never forget.

He turned to me, and we had this conversation.

George:  John, the most important thing here is when you're in a low mood just try not to f*** up your life.

John:  Is that all you've got to say, George?  Do you mean I don't need to try harder to change my mood?

George:  Yeah, that's exactly what I'm saying. Just remember that John. And you will be OK.

When I spoke to Dr. Pransky about this further, his recommendation was as follows.

"John when you're in a low mood just try not to screw up your life so that when you're in a high mood again, you can just get back on track. Just wait for your thinking to change. It always does. You're designed this way."

In low moods, problems that might seem gigantic can look tiny when you are in a higher mood.

In a low mood, we feel very insecure, sensitive and vulnerable and often react aggressively as we don't have the usual balance that we would have otherwise. When you're in a high mood you can see more clearly and therefore there are more possibilities open to you. You take problems much less seriously.

You can take your time and see things more from a bird's eye view. This is a time when it's good to talk to your partner about how to have a nice life together. When you're in a low mood don't do anything that you might regret later when you're in a better mood. Otherwise, you will be so busy picking up the pieces from your low mood that you might go back into another low mood. And so, the cycle continues. Please don't let that happen.

In a nutshell, if you want to have a good relationship, it is important to differentiate between the issues you have, (or think you have), and the moods that you are in when you're living together.

When we are in a high mood, we are in a state of healthy psychological functioning. In other words, this is a natural state which people are in when they are neither in a high nor low mood. In this mood, you are well-balanced, open, warm, and loving.

When two people live in this optimistic state, they have a good basis for a great relationship.

Their personal analytical, fast, thinking has become quiet.

Too much thinking can change normally friendly people into argumentative and very difficult Mr. Hyde-like characters. Their Dr. Jekyll side has gone out of the window.

Too much thinking damages good relationships.

Too much thinking turns princes into frogs because it muddies our view of the other person.

In his book, The Relationship Handbook: A Simple Guide to Satisfying Relationships, Dr. Pransky uses a wonderful picture of

Dr. Jekyll and Mr. Hyde to illustrate the importance of moods in relationships.

**Takeaway**

☑ Too much thinking can change normally friendly people into argumentative and very difficult Mr. Hyde-like characters.

## 5. Help with confidence

*"Confidence is a huge success variable."*
Dr. George Pransky

Have you ever wondered what confidence really is?
For ages, I didn't feel very confident at all. Why not? Well, I certainly knew enough. Even though I thought I didn't. People thought I was confident even when I wasn't. So, on the outside at least, I seemed confident.

But I think the reason why I wasn't confident was that I was thinking too much about myself. I was focusing on what other people might be thinking of me. How might they be criticizing me in their minds? What if I made lots of mistakes? How could I live up to my impossible standards?

As you read this, I'm sure you'll notice the stress behind these words.

In contrast, when I feel more confident, I am not really thinking about anything at all.

In a sense, you could say that I'm "out of my mind." That might sound crazy.

But if you know anybody who has natural self-confidence, you know that they don't continually analyse what other people are saying to them. They are just being themselves and enjoying their lives.

However, even confident people sometimes don't feel very confident. And that's because they start to get into their analytical minds again. When our thinking gets too active, we tend to over-analyse things rather than just observing them for what they are. When this low analytical mood subsides, we can go back to our natural confident selves.

**A Fascinating experiment**

A University of Oregon Professor got a group of children together and asked them four simple questions.

Can you dance?
Can you tell a story?
Can you sing?
Can you draw?

Children are good at being confident. So, when the professor asked them, these questions you can guess what they said. They said, "Yes" with great certainty and enthusiasm.

The children's reactions:

| | |
|---|---|
| Can you dance? | **Yes** |
| Can you tell a story? | **Yes** |
| Can you sing? | **Yes** |
| Can you draw? | **Yes** |

Yes, we can do all of these.

Some years later, the same people, (now young adults) were asked the same question. And the results were very different. It appears, between childhood and young adulthood, they had lost confidence in their ability to do any of these things.

So, what was going on here?

The young adults had started to judge everything they did according to societal standards. Their personal thinking made them conscious of not being able to do things well enough – of falling short in some way.

This is at the core of low confidence.

As adults, we think that our confidence is dependent upon various factors like our experience, our expertise or our level of success, and so on. But children don't have any of these factors. They have no expertise, and they have no experience in anything.

As adults, we tend to do things for self-glorification or self-expansion. We want to get something out of whatever we do. Adults just think too much. Children are different. Children just do things because they just want to do them. They play because they like to play. They sing because they like to sing. And they dance because they like to dance. They are not yet stuck on any judgment as to whether they can do these things or not. Just as in the Nike advertisement, they "just do it." So children already have this natural self-confidence because they've never been taught how not to be confident.

For us to be confident we need to let go of our judgments. We need to get a calm mind. My advice? Just give it a try and see what happens.  Just do things for the sake of enjoyment.

If you play the banjo and enjoy it, just play your banjo and have fun! Even if you play it badly, then just enjoy playing your banjo badly ☺

Don't keep measuring how well you play. It's not good for your confidence.

So, what I'm suggesting here is to revert to that childlike mind you had in your younger years. It will serve you better than overthinking and judging whether you are doing things well enough or not.

As Jesus said, albeit in a different context... "Become as a little child..." Matthew 18.3

**Takeaway**

☑ Judgement is the basis of low confidence. The young adults had started to judge everything they did according to societal standards. Their personal thinking made them conscious of not being able to do things well enough – of falling short in some way.

## 6.  Help with stress

*"The hurrier I go, the behinder I get." (behinder here means further behind)*
Lewis Carroll in Alice in Wonderland

I love the picture of the stressed rabbit in Alice in Wonderland.

The story is a wonderful allegory about the stressful events that happen to Alice and the other characters in Alice in Wonderland.

They are all set in motion by the ***type A behaviour of the White Rabbit.

NOTE ***"type A" managers/people are those who are always trying to do as much as they can in as little time as possible. They tend to create an atmosphere of high stress wherever they go. Maybe you know somebody like this.

If the White Rabbit were taken to a psychiatrist, he might be diagnosed as being a bit mad or even schizophrenic. He would no doubt be branded as a crazy rabbit and be taken away by men (or white rabbits) in white coats.

From what we have learned so far in this book, however, the White Rabbit's "apparent problem" is only caused by his misunderstanding as to where his experience of life comes from. He is not actually a crazy rabbit but rather a misguided one.

Do you recognize yourself in the White Rabbit story? I certainly do.

### Let's hear from the medical expert, Dr. Pettit

I was honored to be taught by Dr. Bill W. Pettit. Dr. Pettit was one of the first people to be trained by Sydney Banks.

Bill is an incredibly experienced and wise psychiatrist who absolutely believes in the potential of everybody to enjoy mental health.

He has witnessed incredible changes in people as a result of insights they have had. After they had these insights, they reached a deep understanding of how their thoughts influence their lives.

In our Zoom meetings, Bill recognized that my mind was practically always in overdrive.

I was a highly professional analyser of everything. I still do this sometimes I must admit. But not nearly so often. I still have crazy white rabbit tendencies, but luckily, I can recognize them earlier than I did before and allow for them accordingly. I am not generally as crazy as I used to be. However, to confirm this last comment - I suggest you ask my friends!

Bill explained to me the far-reaching consequences of these thoughts swirling around in my head. They had a direct result on my feelings. (Remember that our feelings and our thoughts are like two sides of the same coin). And my feelings affected my nervous system. It triggered the equivalent of the caveman being chased by a very hungry saber-toothed tiger – a serious and very stressful situation.

Although this might sound funny, there is a very serious point to it. If this goes on for too long it can have an irreparable effect on our bodies. A high level of stress is no laughing matter.

You might ask, "what can we do about it?" The more we try to analyse what's happening and to get rid of the stress, the stronger it becomes.

In a sense, stress is just an idea.

However, when we have an idea that we are stressed, this thought can develop a life of its own.

This then has a direct effect on our nervous system and causes all sorts of things to happen. These include increased blood pressure, heart problems, reaching for the next packet of cigarettes, or looking for the spirits in the drinks cabinet. None of these can be recommended.

The antidote to all these problems is the same.

It is the understanding that when our minds are bombarded by thinking we need to take a break, relax and calm down. Don't allow yourself to be hijacked by our society's very strong magnetic attraction to becoming a go-getter.

**Takeaway**

☑ The more we try to analyse what's happening and attempt to get rid of the stress, the stronger it becomes.

## 7. Help with money

Money has a real "charge" to it, doesn't it?

We often worry about it a lot. When we have a lot of it, we worry. When we have none of it, we worry. And when we have less than we think we need, we worry.

All this worrying is definitely not good for us.

For many people, money is not seen as a unit of exchange for goods that we require, but as something to achieve emotional support.

As we've heard earlier, rich people are very often not happy. And poor people are sometimes the happiest people you will ever meet.

Sometimes paradoxically, we may feel so attached to money that we actually push it away from us.

It's not the money itself that is important but our thinking which is attached to it.

If we see money as a type of oxygen it can be dangerous. Especially if you don't have any.

Money and our thoughts

How we think about money strongly influences whether we have any money or not. What we believe and think about money is not our fault. It's the result of societal conditioning

which is strongly affected by those people who spend most of our time with us when we grow up. We have no influence over who we have had as our parents or who we have grown up with. Nevertheless, these beliefs are important in determining whether we attract money or repel it, whether we feel okay with having money or not.

Our thinking about money strongly affects the feelings that we have towards it. So, if we think badly about money, we get bad feelings that are associated with those thoughts. These bad feelings affect what we do about trying to acquire money. If we have been raised to feel badly about money, and we get a job, then our actions will not be focused on generating a very high income. Expressions like "money is the root of all evil" strengthen the belief that creating more money is not a good thing to do.

A good friend of mine had the insight that his thinking about money was generated by his upbringing. When he understood this, he realized that his thinking was stopping him from having a good income. When he recognized this, his thinking changed. He started to see money more neutrally.

This new, more helpful attitude towards money paradoxically helped him to generate more of it. His non-attachment to money helped him to feel more relaxed about the whole topic of wealth.

In his wonderful book "Follow your Heart", Andrew Matthews explains that when people have very strong emotions about money, they lose control. Attachment to money, which the Buddhists call "grasping" explains why many people struggle to make any.

"Nature doesn't understand desperation! Nature seeks balance, and you can't be desperate and balanced."

Anonymous author

In his book Creating Affluence: The A-to-Z Steps to a Richer Life, Deepak Chopra refers to wealth consciousness. Wealth consciousness is the feeling that people have when their thoughts about money are unlimited.

I personally think it's also possible for people to feel wealthy even if they don't have a lot of money.

Feeling wealthy is an inside job.

Deepak Chopra says, "truly wealthy people never worry about losing their money because they know that wherever the money comes from there is an inexhaustible supply of it."

What he means is that these wealthy people have an inner sense of knowing that they will have enough money to meet their needs.

Money then is a very subjective thing. And how we feel about it is much more important than how much money we have in the bank.

Material gratification is external, but happiness is internal.

As we grow up, we often learn just the opposite. We might have been brainwashed into thinking that outside objects can make us happy.

This doesn't work. I've already tried it. And so have millions and millions and millions of other people.

In the book Think Like a Monk: The secret of how to harness the power of positivity and be happy now by Jay Shetty, there is a story that illustrates happiness.

It is the story of the musk deer, a tale derived from a poem by Kabir, a fifteenth-century Indian mystic and poet. The musk deer picks up an irresistible scent in the forest and chases it, searching for the source, not realizing that the scent comes from its own pores. It spends its whole life wandering fruitlessly and wondering where the source of the scent is.

In the same way, we search for happiness, finding it impossible to achieve unless we look within ourselves.

This is the case with all material things and money is just one example of these.

"Money, money, money" might make the world go around as in Abba's greatest hit. However, it certainly does not buy happiness.

**Takeaway**

☑    Feeling wealthy is an inside job.

**Resources**
Follow your Heart by Andrew Matthews
This book has beautiful cartoon drawings to accompany Andrew's very wise messages.

## 8. Help with fear and insecurity

Fear is a very common emotion and if it is not managed, it can be totally immobilizing.

One of the powerful outcomes of understanding about the Three Principles is that it helps you to transform fear-generating thoughts into calmer, more stable thoughts. In this new state, fear is reduced or eliminated.

**Gabriela and the rat**

The story of Gabriela and the rats describes just how potent the Three Principles can be **in connection with fear.**

## Gabriela's experience

When Gabriela was even younger, she learned to be afraid of rats. Her mother was afraid of rats, so she learned this fear from her mother.

Now I have her written version of how she experienced the "rat incident." I decided to set it up as though we were having an interview about the rat.

**I am in the role of the interviewer and Gabriela is answering.**

G = Gabriela | J = John

J:      Thanks for agreeing to our interview Can you say a few words about your experience of fear of rats?

G:      I would describe my fear more as a paralyzing phobia that produced terrifying feelings.

J:      Did you try to do anything about it?

G:      Yes, I had tried to resolve this phobia because it was very uncomfortable.

J:      You talked to me briefly about this rat. What happened?

G:      The incident with the rat climbing my arm was before seeing the movie. I entered someone's house and the rat was on his back legs...it looked like a brown squirrel, minus the tale.  When I realized that it was a rat I felt panic but then I noticed that I was ok when I thought it was a squirrel.  This experience gave me hope and made me curious about the power of thought.

J: So the "squirrel "did not freak you out but the rat did? It was exactly the same animal, but it caused a totally different reaction. And then you saw this great movie, Ratatouille. Right?

G: Yes, I was showing the movie to kids at Juvenile Hall.

J: And after that you felt different?

G: Yes.

J: In what way? "

G: I saw that rats and mice are creatures like any other living creature, just another expression of LIFE.

J: Is that the end of the story?

G: No, not quite. After the movie incident I saw a something at the bottom of a pool. At first, I thought it was a leaf...no fear, but then my mind got creative and thought it was a rat. My heart started palpitating faster...but not as before. I actually "saw" a rat. Then I looked again and saw the leaf. Fear left me. These three insights have transformed my experience of rodents from PHOBIA to acceptance and at time discomfort. For me this was life changing.

J: Thanks so much Gabriela.

G: My pleasure.


We can from this story very clearly see how our way of seeing outside events has a dramatic effect on our internal feelings.

This effect is happening every moment of every day.

**Takeaway**

- ☑ Rats have a very bad name. They are not intrinsically horrible creatures.
- ☑ I know someone who loves rats and even keeps one at home! We are all very different.

### 9. Help with avoiding suicide

As I was making the final changes to this book,

I saw a heart-wrenching report on television.

In this report, three men did a huge 300-mile walk to earn money for a charity to prevent suicide in young people.

Each of these men had had daughters and all their daughters had committed suicide.

One of the men from Greater Manchester, lost his daughter in March 2020.

He said: "My daughter hated the fact that she could not finish college with her friends and saw all her plans being cancelled one by one."

The second of the three men lost his 18-year-old, daughter too. She also passed away in March 2020 after trying to take her own life.

"Had she just taken time to think or to speak to someone, her decision and my family's lives would be on another path," her father said: "I strongly believe that in a moment of darkness my daughter made a wrong decision."

The third of the trio lost her daughter when she took her own life on 19 December 2018, shortly after separating from her husband.

She was due to return home a day later for the festive season and had taken a lease on a 'lovely apartment', after just having been offered a new position at work. She seemed excited about her new job according to her father.

The trio hopes that their 'extraordinary journey' will raise awareness for suicide prevention and will spare other families the agony of losing a child.

The fathers have so far raised more than £300,000 for their charity.

This charity is to support schools in helping them to provide education to young people who are thinking about suicide.

This national television report which I saw had a great impact on me and so I wanted to add this important section to the ways in which the Three Principles can help people.

I have, of course, taken out the names of the 3 fathers and have reported on them anonymously.

From my own experience, I know that my thoughts, when infused with consciousness, can have so much power over me. They appear so real. They are so real that they tempt us to act.

Understanding just a little bit about where my experience of life comes from has helped me to get a small distance from my thoughts. This had certainly helped me when I was planning to do horrible things to myself. The distance and the more objective perspective I got on my thinking helped me to see that maybe these thoughts were in fact "just" thoughts.

**Takeaway**

☑ From my own experience, I know that my thoughts, when infused with consciousness, can have so much power over me. They appear so real. They are so real that they tempt us to act.

## 10. Help with Coaching, Training and Counselling

### Dr Pransky and his special teaching of the 3 principles

### On 1st June 2022, 18.00 CET

I was so pleased I attended an inspiring meeting with 63 coaches who work in the field of coaching. They are interested in exploring further how and why the Three Principles helps people to see how they experience their world.

The occasion was the release of a wonderful book by my friend Sheela Masand.

Dr Pransky, (Jack) was one of the people featured in this book where Sheela had invited Jack to do one of 13 interviews with Three Principles aficionados. All of these 13 people had worked directly with Sydney Banks. They had received these learnings directly from these wonderful teachers.

Sheela had asked him his views on coaching people from the understanding of the 3 Principles.

The day was 31st May 2022, 11.00 CET. The previous day, on 31st May at 11.00 am I had spoken to a wonderful person, a highly qualified coach called Sharaf. In fact, I would consider him to be a new friend.

Sharaf, (who is from Cairo) although I have only known him for 7 weeks or so, I do not say this lightly. Friends to me are very special.

We met on Zoom, as Sharaf was interested in having a close look at the language we need to coach effectively. I was meeting him as a colleague and friend, not as in the typical coach-client relationship.

In our coaching session Sharaf coached me. What we both noticed is that when his mind was free, then I, as the "client," felt a strong connection with Sharaf as the coach.

Sometimes, however, I noticed that this connection became a lot weaker. At the end of our session, I was curious to ask him what he had felt. His answer was fascinating and, in my view, shows his experience as a coach and his depth of self-reflection. He said that he had been having a lot of ideas as to how he could help me. He was formulating questions in his mind as I was trying to articulate what I wanted to say. It was then that he noticed that the connection we had become weaker.

We noticed that three of the criteria for the highest level of coaching training available

(MCC level-Master Coach) they are aimed at creating a similar atmosphere to what Jack was describing above. Here they are.

The section in the handbook is called:

Coaching Presence (MCC Examination Handbook).

Here are some of the paragraphs which describe the criteria which the coaches need to pass the examination.

4.1 - The coach is an empathetic observer, completely connected to the client as a whole being and to what wants to unfold through him/her.

4.3 - The coach is in a complete partnership with the client where the client is an equal or greater contributor to the conversation and the direction of the coaching than the coach. There is a field of resonance between coach-client.

4.11 - The coach trusts completely the inherent value of the coaching process and does not need to create value.

Now let me turn back to the meeting on the following day with Jack, Sheela and the other 60 or so coaches.

In this magical meeting, Jack explained his experience of supporting people with the 3 Principles over his long career. It can be crystalized into a 4-step process which we he uses for all coaching situations.

1. **We are in our own health**
   Some of us do not realize or remember this. In other words, there is nothing wrong with us. Traditional therapy is based on the fact that we have stuff to fix.

2. **People come to us (as coaches) with "a lot of stuff on their mind."**
   Clarity is clouded by a lot of thinking. This makes it hard for us to think straight or come up with creative solutions. If we as coaches are able to help our coachees to relax so that her thoughts settle, then this is great. It creates the room for new thoughts to bubble up.

3. **Deep listening – Nothing on my mind**
   This is the most important skills or state for us to learn. An empty mind.
   A blank book. As Jack calls it, "an empty vessel."
   I love this metaphor. It suggests that, like a boat, which can carry and support its cargo, with its natural buoyancy, so the coach or mentor can support the coachee. The coachee is safe because of the boat's natural buoyancy which the water always provides.

4.  **I do not know mode.**
    We approach coaching as a kind of exploration in which we, as coaches, look for signals that we are moving in the right direction. Jack describes this as "getting a hit." He is suddenly "hit by an idea" which he then explores with his partner. We do not come with a preconceived notion of what the coachees challenge is. (Sometimes therapists refer to this as a "presenting illness." And this title clearly suggests that there is something fundamentally wrong with the client)

**If you are feeling low or unhappy.**

When I was feeling down in the dumps, I noticed a dramatic difference between the atmosphere of a traditional therapist and a Three Principles coach. There was an attitude of hope and exploring together rather than one of resignation and fixing with drugs

Jack has not quite yet retired. For me and many other people this long, extended semi-retirement period is great as we continue to get to see Jack in action!

**Takeaway**

☑   Clarity is clouded by a lot of thinking. This makes it hard for us to think straight or come up with creative solutions. If we as coaches are able to help those people who we coach to relax so that her thoughts settle, then this is great. It creates the room for new thoughts to bubble up.

## 11. Help with Learning

*The emphasis on mindsets, on resilience, on "Educator, heal thyself" speaks to the heart of matters.*

John Hattie, Author of Visible Learning

Quoted by Ami Chen-Naim Mills and Roger C. Mills Ph.D. in their wonderful book, "State of Mind in the Classroom"

Have you ever been reading a book and after you turn the page you realise that you have no idea what you have just been reading about? I certainly have.

This is quite common. Our thinking is working continually whether we like it or not. Trying to ban it from our minds is counterproductive. When you try to block thoughts by telling them to go away, they fight back. They return like a well-trained homing pigeon. That is why affirmations do not work very well.

Our challenge here is one of our mindset or state of mind. Great learners have a relaxed, almost meditative state of mind. Not such good learners have a mind which is flitting from one to thing to the next, almost like a butterfly that often quickly moves from one object to another.

As kids we tried to get a butterfly to land on our arm. The less you did the better. We tried to run after the butterfly. However, our best strategy was always to keep quiet and not to move.

Paradoxically, it is the same when learning anything.
Calmness is a huge factor in learning effectively.

There are a number of other factors which help learning and there are also factors which hinder learning. Here are just a few of them.

| Help learning | Hinder Learning |
| --- | --- |
| Fluid Mind set | Fixed mindset |
| Openness | Closed |
| Optimistic | Pessimistic |
| Curious | Bored |
| Arrogance | Humility |
| Relaxed mind | Overactive mind |

**Takeaway**

☑ Calmness is a huge factor in learning effectively.

**Resources**

State of Mind in the Classroom by Ami Chen-Naim Mills and Roger C. Mills Ph.D. A great book about applying these understandings to education.

**Optimism and Sydney Banks**

Sydney Banks was always a great advocate of optimism.

But why?

Before I answer this question let us look at a bit of research from

**"The Guardian*(please see below) newspaper"**

"Scientists found that while optimists reacted to, and recovered from, stressful situations in much the same way as pessimists, the optimists fared better emotionally because they had fewer stressful events in their daily lives.

How optimists minimize their dose of stress is unclear, but the researchers believe they either avoid arguments, lost keys, traffic jams and other irritations, or simply fail to perceive them as stressful in the first place."

From what we have talked about so far, my view is different. Optimists (and those who understand the principles which I have written about here) well know that these "lost keys, traffic jams and other irritations" have a potential to be stressful. However, because they know that our thoughts continually come and go, they do not get so upset when bad things happen.

**\*The Guardian**

Here is some research from a report in the Guardian newspaper, a much-respected source of daily news in the UK

These bad feelings which affect us go away automatically when our thinking changes. In life we cannot avoid bad things happening. If we see how the process works and if we know that these bad feelings are temporary, then we naturally feel more positive and hopeful.

A general attitude of optimism, the feeling that things are going to work out well, makes sense if you want a happier life.

There are positive and negative types of thoughts which mold the direction of our lives.

Here are 2 examples. *This is not going to work.* This type of thought creates a feeling of hopelessness if it is continually repeated. *This will work out somehow.* This creates a feeling of hopefulness if it becomes your most common type of thoughts.

These thoughts then become embodied in our physiology bodies, and we genuinely feel our thoughts. They are real to us.

Thoughts cannot hurt you even though they sometimes feel as though they can. They can have tremendous power over us.

*"Positive thoughts create a healthy mind and a stable life. Optimism is a spiritual quality and a guiding light that will lead you to happiness."*

Sydney Banks in his book, the Missing Link

**There is always hope**

You might feel that there is no way out. But, in fact, there is always a way out. It is helpful if you have someone by your side to help you to see this for yourself. There is a way to feel happier again. I know that this is true because I have personally experienced it.

*There is nothing either good or bad but thinking makes it so.* William Shakespeare

**On thinking**

We often try to analyse our thinking. Sometimes it's just better to wait until our hectic, repetitive, and negative thinking calms down. Thoughts always change. New thoughts replace the old ones. You can be 100% sure of that.

It's as simple as that. This is how it works.

We often look for complex solutions where a simple answer is "hiding." Sydney Banks told a wonderful story to illustrate this.

Sherlock Holmes and Dr. Watson had just finished a case successfully and went into the countryside to relax. They decided to spend the time camping. They were just lying down to have a good night's sleep when Sherlock Homes asked Watson – "Watson, what do you notice?"

Watson enthusiastically described the sky and the stars and the constellations– the great bear, the plow, and the enormity of space...the almost spiritual feeling of being one with the universe... This sophisticated, philosophical speech went on for ages and ages.

Finally, Dr. Watson stopped and turned to Sherlock Holmes and asked: *"What do you notice Sherlock?"*

Sherlock Holmes replied. It is very simple Watson,
*"Someone has stolen our tent."*

This is a wonderful story that reminds us that very often we do not notice the simple things in our lives. We get so caught up in complexity that we are blind to simple and important truths.

We tend to take ourselves much too seriously. That has often been the case in my life.

I briefly mentioned Michael Singer earlier in this book. I love how Michael Singer puts life (here on earth) into perspective.

### "We are spinning on a planet..."

"Walk outside on a clear night and just look up into the sky. You are sitting on a planet spinning around in the middle of absolutely nowhere.

Though you can only see a few thousand stars, there are hundreds of billions of stars in our Milky Way alone. In fact, it is estimated that there are over a trillion stars in the Spiral Galaxy. And that galaxy would look like one star to us if we could even see it. You're just standing on one little ball of dirt and spinning around one of the stars. From that perspective, do you really care what people think about your clothes or your car? Do you really need to feel embarrassed if you forget someone's name?

How can you let these meaningless things cause pain? If you want out, if you want a decent life, you had better not devote your life to avoiding

psychological pain. You had better not spend your life worrying about whether people like you or whether your car impresses people."

## We can always choose which train to take

Imagine you're standing at a railway station, and you see that the next train is not your favourite. It looks really dirty and is full of people who are standing like sardines in the aisles.

Would you get on this train?

Would it really make sense, especially as other trains will come a few minutes later? Our thoughts are a bit like this. We are waiting at the "station of thoughts" and trains of thought come past all the time.

Imagine an unpleasant thought coming into the station.

We can choose whether we get onto this train or not. If we get on it, we will feel the effect of the thoughts, and these might not be very nice feelings. And if we realize this we can get off at the next station.

Or, if we are feeling sporty, we can jump off!

**Like the guy in this illustration above, we can choose when to get off our train of thought**

In my life, I've often stayed on the train of negative thoughts for much too long. Now, at least, I actually notice that I'm on this horrible train. Thankfully, now I often get off at the next station. This makes my life a lot easier. Not perfect, just easier.

Let's not get on the next train if we don't want to. If we see that we are on the wrong train, then jump off as soon as possible.

**Enjoy your life and don't be afraid of your experiences**

I spent many, many years on the hamster wheel of life. I was always doing stuff faster, better, more effectively. But doing more stuff did not make me feel better. It just took my mind off my life for a short time.

So, as you get to the end of this book, I would like to remind you to relax and enjoy the journey of life.

Feel free not to try to work hard at learning about this understanding. The understanding

of how life works. Just read these words as though you are listening to a wonderful concert performed by your favourite artist.

**Be suspicious of your thoughts**

Happy people are suspicious of their negative thoughts. Happy people naturally understand how their thinking works.

I wish I had heard of this secret when I was 9 years old.

Thinking can be very tricky. It can trick us into thinking almost anything. It can trick us into thinking that we are useless or a waste of space. Or it can trick us into thinking that we are the best footballer in the world... that we are rich or poor or happy or sad or depressed or filled with joy.

Happy people do not believe their thinking so readily. When their inner voice tells them how unhappy they are and how hopeless their life is, then they become a bit suspicious.

They say to themselves...

"My life is basically the same as it was yesterday. And now I feel terrible.

How does this make sense? It cannot be anything to do with my outside circumstances. Maybe I am being tricked, again by my own very sly thinking!"

My dad was a naturally happy person and he believed in common sense. When he was off form, as he called it, he always knew or felt it was short-term. He did not believe everything his thoughts were telling him.

He called it common sense. He, like Sydney Banks, said that it is only logical that you feel good when you have happy thoughts and sad when you have unhappy thoughts. It is important to remember that you do not need to try to change these thoughts. Our thoughts come and go continually.

They will go away on their own just like dark clouds drift by in the ever-changing sky. The countryside will become bathed in sun once again just as soon as the clouds have dispersed.

It is not rocket science Sydney Banks used to say. And he was right.

I really hope it helps you to have a more joyful life. Thank you for joining me on our journey.

Let me finish with a quotation from the man himself, Sydney Banks, who we can all thank for sharing these wonderful insights with us and the whole world.

*If the only thing people learned, was not to be afraid of their experience, that alone would change the world.*

Sydney Banks

**Takeaway**

- ☑ Do not believe your thoughts
- ☑ Remember that you can choose to get off the train of crappy thoughts if you want to
- ☑ Remember that we are a part of one gigantic universal whole

**Resources**

All Michael Singer's books are excellent in my view.
CD course - By Michael Singer

# Acknowledgments

Thank you to a very large number of people who have kindly supported me through thick and thin over the years.

To my mum and dad who loved and supported me in all that I have done, wherever I did it and unconditionally.

Michaela (Michili) Plewik who I love very much. She is also very patient. ☺

My brother, Richard and his wife Liz who have always been there when I have needed them.

Christiane Neuss who I have known since I arrived in Germany 40 years ago! You have helped me more than you could ever imagine.

Jack Pransky whose support has been priceless. Thank you so much Jack.

Gabriela Maldonada Montano,
 my wonderful friend who I have enjoyed discussing many topics I write about in this book for many hours. Without Gabriela I would never have finished this book.

Sheela, who convinced me to go to a seminar in Spain. This course was for me the start of a very transformational part of my life.

Katja, whose endless patience and willingness to chat to me, whenever I call is wonderful.

Declan for his wonderful sense of humor and his patient attempts to help me with my golf swing.

Dr George Pransky. Thank you, George for 7 unforgettable days in La Conner.

Michael Neill who really got me started on the road to understanding how life works. I did not finish your course, but my penny eventually dropped. Thanks Michael.

Steve Chandler. It is wonderful to have you as a friend, Steve. Thanks so much for your help!

Dr Bill Pettit who reminded me that no one is broken including me.

Dr Amy Johnson. Thanks for your great coaching, Amy.

Mick Tomlinson for your friendship and willingness to help me with my wonderfully intuitive and sometimes puzzling Apple computer.

Kevin thanks for teaching me so much about apple computers and showing me how to set up a professional online presentation using the very latest ideas. Magic.

Andrew Bridgewater for our great coaching sessions.

Dr Stähle, the only traditional therapist who I have ever met who really listens deeply.

Dr Angela Scarano, my very special Italian friend. Thank you for our beautiful friendship.

Mark Russell who I love spending my time with. You are a great friend Mark. Thank you for listening.

Christoph Kopp, a super coach.

Ken Taylor, a brilliant teacher and great friend.

Bill Cummings for his love and encouragement.

Claudia and David Law for being friends for so many years.

Howard for his wonderful coaching. I am so pleased that I met you. When we speak I feel connected to you even though we live on opposite sides of the globe.

Katy Peacey, who I enjoyed chatting to and laughing with so much over breakfast in Spain. She is sadly no longer with us but I will never forgot you Katy.

Xi Ding, from China, living in Vienna, a wonderful caricaturist who patiently taught me the beauty of learning how to draw caricatures. His patience was unbelievable. My caricatures are a "work in progress."

Matto for his great support in teaching me how to translate my ideas into simple drawings. His help was invaluable and enabled me to illustrate this book. Thank you very much Matto.

Thank you to Carole for her patience in helping me to knock this manuscript into shape so that it actually looks like a book. I have really enjoyed our light-hearted and I have learned a lot from you in our meetings. Thank you.

**Anybody else?**

If I have forgotten anyone important, please excuse me☺.

**Here are some other great books**

1. Creating the Teachable Moment by Darlene L. Stewart
2. One Thought Changes Everything by Mara Gleason
3. The Huge Bag of Worries by Virginia Ironside
   This book includes some lovely illustrations by Fank Rodger
4. LITA la frijolita y la asombrosa aventura del globo de chicle
   Spanisch Ausgabe | von Antonio Luis Gómez Molero, Pablo
   Ortega López, et al. | 28. September 2017
   (Spanish Edition) Kindle Edition
   Editors: Contee Seely– Gabriela Maldonado-Montano
5. Just a Thought: A No-Willpower Approach to Overcome Self-Doubt and Make Peace with Your Mind by Dr Amy Johnson
6. Creating the Impossible: A 90-day Program to Get Your Dreams Out of Your Head and into the World, by Michael Neill
7. You can feel good again - Common-Sense Strategies for Releasing Unhappiness and Changing your life
8. Coming Home by Dicken Bettinger and Nataska Swerdloff
9. What if your already knew the answers to your questions? By Elsie Spittle
10. Clarity: Clear Mind, Better Performance, Bigger Results by Jamie Smart
11. Somebody should have told us by Jack Pransky
12. The Seven Spiritual Laws of Success by Deepak Chopra
13. Awareness by Anthony de Mello

# A few words about me

I really love teaching people how to feel better about and I would love to get to know you personally.

I have a simple goal in life. My aim for everyone who I meet is that they feel a little bit better than they did before they met me. This is especially true for those people who feel sad, depressed and lonely, as I did before I understood something about the ideas in this book.

As a reformed introvert who used to be unbelievably shy, my aim is to help people to speak in front of a group confidently and memorably so that they can communicate their important message with joy, fun and enthusiasm.

I think that we can all influence the world in a positive way.

# Contact

**Website**
www.johndoorbar.com

**Email**
If you wish, then please contact me
johndoorbar@ece-euro.de

**Phone**
0049 173 90 399 49

Ingram Content Group UK Ltd.
Milton Keynes UK
UKHW020626240423
420680UK00015B/752

9 783756 879717